The Sorcerer

Stephen Shaw

The Sorcerer

ISBN: 978-0-9928042-9-9

Stephen Shaw's Books

Visit the website: www.i-am-stephen-shaw.com

I Am contains spiritual and mystical teachings from enlightened masters that point the way to love, peace, bliss, freedom and spiritual awakening.

Heart Song takes you on a mystical adventure into creating your reality and manifesting your dreams, and reveals the secrets to attaining a fulfilled and joyful life.

They Walk Among Us is a love story spanning two realities. Explore the mystery of the angels. Discover the secrets of Love Whispering.

The Other Side explores the most fundamental question in each reality. What happens when the physical body dies? Where do you go? Expand your awareness. Journey deep into the Mystery.

Reflections offers mystical words for guidance, meditation and contemplation. Open the book anywhere and unwrap your daily inspiration.

5D is the Fifth Dimension. Discover ethereal doorways hidden in the fabric of space-time. Seek the advanced mystical teachings.

Star Child offers an exciting glimpse into the future on earth. The return of the gods and the advanced mystical teachings. And the ultimate battle of light versus darkness.

The Tribe expounds the joyful creation of new Earth. What happened after the legendary battle of Machu Picchu? What is Christ consciousness? What is Ecstatic Tantra?

The Fractal Key reveals the secrets of the shamans. This handbook for psychonauts discloses the techniques and practices used in psychedelic healing and transcendent journeys.

Stephen Shaw's Books

Atlantis illuminates the Star Beings and Earth's Ancient History. A magical history ingrained in your deepest consciousness, in your myths and mysteries. Discover the secret teachings of the star beings.

The Sorcerer is a journey into Magick, Power and Mysticism. Discover the Twelve Auspicious Symbols. Explore the paths of Awareness, Love and Tantra. Absorb the sacred teachings and mantras of the lamas.

You just know this is going to be a different kind of book.

If you have got this far through the mystical series, then you are going to feel right at Home.

If you are starting out, then may I suggest you begin with the iconic book I Am, and gradually wade through the rest of the books, taking your time to absorb the layered lessons and unearth the hidden gems.

It's best to keep your heart and mind wide open. Absorb the spiritual energy. Immerse deeply in the story.

Oh yeah ... my books are designed to be read at a slower, meditative pace.

It's kinda fun when you get the hang of it.

* * *

I have always been interested in books. My mother had us reading from an early age. Dad used to play those large reel-to-reel music tapes, containing hours of music. He was a social animal, organising parties and BBQs around our shimmering

1

pool. We even had outside speakers, so good vibes accompanied us in the expansive garden.

But I digress.

It's those delicious words floating on white pages that intrigued me, captivated me. Books are magical creatures ... kind of alive ... the texture and aesthetic of the covers ... the pages turning beneath your fingers ... the transmission of energy and light and colourful imagination.

I guess it was inevitable that I would become a collector of these marvellous tomes.

My small home is pretty much an overflowing library. There are shelves, but not enough to contain the bustling volumes. I ought to get more organised. Dust is my constant companion. And soft light. I adore soft light. I open the windows often to circulate fresh air, but the curtains remain half drawn.

Outdoors is for healthy sunlight, for recharging the body and invigorating the psyche. Indoors is for calming light, for relaxing and perusing. I read somewhere that when the sun goes down, you should avoid blue light (typically emanating from computer screens, televisions and cell phones); instead you should switch to red or amber light, which increases melatonin production. Naturally, that suits me. Soothing red light fills my home in the evenings. My eyes feel gently caressed during reading sessions, and I sleep deeply and restfully every night.

Being a modern man, I often read books via the Kindle app on my large cell phone. Obviously this is ideal when travelling. The secret is to download a blue-light filter for your phone. Be kind to your eyes and brain. You are going to need them as you live your wonderful life.

Yep, I love travelling.

It is my other passion.

Mother was a free spirit, a flower-child of the '60s. Did I inherit her genes? Was it infused in my essence? I don't know. Dad said "Work hard. Be sensible. Take responsibility." Mom said "Travel. Explore. Be free."

Sadly, she died when I was very young.

* * *

So here I am.

Standing before yet another glass door.

Lost Horizon Bookstore in Santa Barbara, California, proffers a select stock of antiquarian, rare and used books in many fields. (Antiquarian means 'relating to or studying antiques, rare books or antiquities' according to the Oxford Concise English Dictionary.) It is also a good place to find antique maps, vintage posters and fine leather-bound books.

Yummy.

It is still early in the morning. I scrutinise the tantalising window merchandise ... slowly savouring every delicious moment ... eventually pushing open the door and entering the glorious sanctuary.

No one here except me and the owner. Perfect.

We exchange cordial greetings. I make my way to the California History section. When in a new location, it is good to learn about its past. Yesteryear has always fascinated me.

I scan the array of varicoloured titles. Taking my sweet time …

Large book on the very top shelf. Gleaming, with a hint of dust. Ah … it's a stretch but I can just reach.

Dark green swirling cover. No title. Heavy in my hands. Intriguing.

I sit on a nearby chair. Run my fingers along the ornate purple stitching. The book suddenly flips open.

Everything becomes dark.

Disoriented and confused.

Air is musty. My voice echoes.

What on earth is happening?

Roisterous laughter reverberates.

Who dares rouse the magick book?

A figure striding toward me. Long purple coat flaring, almost-black combat boots crunching. Unkempt, shoulder-length dark hair wafting in an invisible breeze. Streaks of grey across the temples. Radiant green eyes.

Up close and personal.

Hairs on my arms are bristling.

"Uh … Where am I?"

Wrong question.

I feel the hand upon my chest.

Rough thrust, back to my reality.

In the bookstore, coughing and spluttering.

The owner looks at me curiously. "Are you ok? Need some assistance?"

I jump up, waving the book frantically. "What is this?"

He strolls over and gives a cursory glance.

"A Wild Free Horse. First edition. Signed by the author."

The cover is brown. The title is bold. It's not the same book.

Trying not to appear foolish, I retrieve the hardback. "Thank you."

I have no idea what's going on. Pause for a few moments, settle my breathing.

Even though the experience was frightening, I realise something.

I must buy this book.

The transaction is swift. Payment of two hundred dollars. And I am out the door.

A strange sensation tickles my tummy, fostering a smile.

Aware of a single thought trickling into my consciousness.

This book should have been in the Supernatural section.

* * *

There is something else I adore.

Oceans.

That soothing scchhh sound ... soft breeze ruffling my hair ... ebb and flow of the tides ... water caressing my feet on a sunny day ... waves that pound the shore on wintry days ... all its moods ... tempestuous and tranquil.

Stearns Wharf is only a 20-minute walk from the bookstore. It's an invitation my soul cannot refuse.

A beautiful sculpture of leaping dolphins atop a water-filled basin welcomes visitors. Known locally as Dolphin Fountain, its official title is Santa Barbara's Bicentennial Friendship Fountain.

Soon I am ambling past the quaint wooden stores and restaurants. At the end of the wharf, I stand and gaze at the gorgeous Pacific Ocean. In the distance are bobbing yachts and fishing boats. This is pure bliss (rivalled only, perhaps, by sunsets and organic dark chocolate).

The magick book lays next to me on the bench.

I am viewing it with trepidation. Did something mysterious really happen? Was it a substance-induced hallucination? A trick of the light? A brain seizure?

Should I attempt to open it again?

Even in this serene setting I cannot bring myself to do it.

An hour disappears as I meditate on rippling waves. I feel incredibly peaceful and happy.

Eventually I take a slow walk back to the parked rental car.

A sparkle infiltrates my mind.

Booster. Shot of courage. Swirling white foam.

Cup of coffee!

I know what you're thinking. I don't really drink coffee. Even a cup at 10:00 am keeps me up at night. I am easily overstimulated. I remember a previous girlfriend who could drink coffee an hour before bed and sleep easily. Guess we are all different.

In fact, we are all different.

While 'genotype' refers to the genetic constitution of an individual, 'phenotype' refers to the characteristics of an individual resulting from interaction of its genotype with the environment.

Coffee makes me jittery and overthinkative (is that a word?).

Sometimes I need a cappuccino.

Racking my brains.

Dad's spirited words spring sentiently: "When the problem is solved, the solution seems obvious." and "There is always a solution, son."

Aha! Bulletproof Coffee.

I consult my phone. The nearest store is two hours' drive. I can take Route 101 and hug the coast all the way, passing through Ventura and Malibu to reach Main Street, Santa Monica.

As an aside, the health books that changed my life were Effortless Healing and Fat For Fuel by Dr Joseph Mercola. They are in a league of their own. His website is one of the most visited health sites in the world.

The Complete Guide to Fasting by Dr Jason Fung is also essential reading. The benefits of healthy fasting are phenomenal.

However, if you are into biohacking and frontier-pushing nutrition, read The Bulletproof Diet by Dave Asprey. It offers plenty of useful ideas. His bulletproof coffee, of course, is legendary.

Between you and me, I often bulletproof my morning green tea (which is full of healthy catechins and mild caffeine) by adding C8 MCT oil (caprylic acid). The latter raises fat-burning, brain-fuelling molecules in your body called ketones. Oh yeah!

Nutrition is a personal choice. Always do your research, heed medical guidelines, and discover what works best for your body.

As for me, I am destined for a delicious bulletproof coffee.

* * *

There it is.

The famous dove logo.

Oh, did I mention the range of super-nutritious meals on the menu?

Tummy is rumbling. I place an order and relax on a comfy chair.

The magick book is perched safely on my lap.

Bulletproof coffee arrives. Scrumptious lunch follows.

Ah, that special kick. Feeling the surge of energy.

Deep breath. It's now or never.

Scrutinise the green swirling cover.

Run my fingers tentatively along the purple stitching.

The book suddenly flips open.

Everything becomes dark.

Am I in a large cave?

Roisterous laughter again.

Are you sure you want to go down this road?

My neck hairs are prickling.

Nothing but a disembodied voice.

Choose my questions carefully.

"What will happen if I do?"

Your life will be changed forever.

Hesitate. Thinking quickly.

I am 32 years old. Single. No children. I relish knowledge and crave adventure.

"Is this good or evil?"

This is the Path of Light.

"How do I know if you are being truthful?"

Ignore your fear. Follow your Heart.

Sigh. Biting my bottom lip.

What have I got to lose?

I nod cautiously.

A picture is appearing on the open page.

Luminous white conch shell.

Remember, you always have free will.

Feel compelled to place my hand upon it.

Palm downward, resting upon the shimmering icon.

Searing heat! Pain shoots up my wrist.

I scream in agony. Severe burning.

After several minutes it subsides.

I gaze at my inner forearm.

A tattoo of a white conch shell.

Welcome to the Path.

Disoriented.

Return to the coffee shop.

No one seems to notice me.

I need to leave. Get some fresh air.

Ocean Front Walk is five minutes away.

A stroll alongside the beach will suit me.

I am alone and there is much to process.

Ocean breeze. Warm sun.

Deep breaths.

Relief.

* * *

I need a simple distraction.

A pause between these intense musical notes.

I don't understand what is happening to me.

Time to take a little detour from this winding path.

I have one more hidden interest. Perhaps a secret passion.

Always had a strong enthusiasm for martial arts.

The fire was stoked by that legend known as Bruce Lee. He took the martial arts world by storm. Initially learning a close-range combat style of Kung Fu called Wing Chun (means 'Spring Chant' or 'Eternal Spring'), he went on to learn, absorb and appropriate a range of fighting techniques from Judo, Western Boxing, Savate and Fencing.

He was interested in efficiency, stripping out uneconomical movements, and keeping only that which was useful. Eventually he amalgamated the best of techniques into his own formidable martial art titled Jeet Kune Do (means 'Way Of The Intercepting Fist').

Let me interject here: I am not a fighter. I am a collector of interesting and intriguing books. I love reading. I am an expert at drinking tea and doing nothing. A sofa is my best friend.

It is the principles of Bruce Lee and Jeet Kune Do which are fascinating. In no particular order: functional efficiency (minimum effort with maximum results); simplicity (only keep what works); directness (not waste time); fluidity (not fixed or rigid); adaptability (flow with the situation).

Those are wonderful principles to apply to life.

Bruce Lee was born in 1940 in San Francisco, California. He became a famous martial artist and film star. Shortly before the release of his film Enter The Dragon, he died at age 32 in 1973.

Unknown to most people, another legend was emerging contemporaneously.

Helio Gracie was born in 1913 in Belem do Para, Brazil. At a young age he learned traditional Japanese Jiu-Jitsu techniques from his older brother Carlos. He soon began to modify those techniques, employing the same principles mentioned above. After years of refinement (similar to Bruce Lee), he proved his art's effectiveness by defeating larger and stronger opponents. His renowned martial art is titled Gracie Jiu-Jitsu (often referred to as Brazilian Jiu-Jitsu or BJJ).

In 1978 Helio's eldest son Rorion Gracie left Brazil to live in the United States. To demonstrate the superiority of Gracie Jiu-Jitsu over other martial arts, he created the Ultimate Fighting Championship (UFC). This pay-per-view platform showcased martial artists of all styles and schools. Rorion's brother Royce used the simplicity and effectiveness of Gracie Jiu-Jitsu to repeatedly win matches, which fostered a worldwide revolution in martial arts. Today, every Mixed Martial Arts (MMA) fighter climbs into an octagon (fighting ring) with a solid working knowledge of Gracie or Brazilian Jiu-Jitsu.

Even if you are not a fighter, regular training in Gracie or Brazilian Jiu-Jitsu contributes to superb strength, fitness, fat-burning and overall body-conditioning. It also provides an excellent grounding in basic self-defence.

Unfortunately my right shoulder was injured in a car accident; otherwise I'd definitely put my books down, get off the sofa, and do weekly Brazilian Jiu-Jitsu classes. Anyway, that's my story and I'm sticking to it.

So, here comes the distraction.

The Gracie Jiu-Jitsu Academy is only 30 minutes' drive from Bulletproof Coffee. It is located in Torrance, California.

I noticed the advertisement near Ocean Front Walk. Rener Gracie is giving a talk this evening on the Principles of Self-Defence. Seems like a great opportunity to learn something new.

After that, I will have dinner then retire to my hotel bed. Tomorrow is another day. Hopefully the magick book will make more sense.

* * *

I slept for a few hours. Now I'm awake.

A dark bedroom is excellent for melatonin production. But it's always unsettling sleeping in a strange room. I generally prefer to leave a night-light in a corner.

Sipping the water at my bedside.

My new tattoo feels itchy. It's glowing in the dark, which is amusing.

Are you ready?

The familiar voice makes me jump.

Try to stay calm and relaxed.

"What's going to happen?"

You're going on a journey.

Suddenly the tattoo explodes into light. The entire room is filled with colourful spinning threads forming a huge vortex. It's both glorious and terrifying.

I look down on the bed and see my body twitching and convulsing.

"Is it going to be alright?"

Let go and surrender.

The body seems to slumber peacefully.

We float up into the vortex. Is that my forearm in front of me? Or a disembodied white conch shell leading the way?

Hovering before an azure glass door.

I have to smile. It's a symbol of my life.

"How do I enter?"

Wave your tattoo. It grants access.

"Aha."

Standing on the other side is a monk. Dressed in a maroon robe and sandals.

He's a lama.

"Oh?"

A lama is a spiritual teacher and wise person. Sometimes a therapist and healer. Often helping the sick and dying.

"Am I dying?"

Not at all.

Prudent pause.

Perhaps a little.

"What does that mean?"

The lama politely beckons. I quietly follow.

Moving through the doorway. My feet touch solid ground. There's a large sign mounted on a beautiful wooden overhang: 'Sera Monastery'.

"Where are we?"

The lama's voice is soft-spoken: "Sera Monastery in Tibet. Nestled at the base of Mount Pubuchok, also known as Tatipu Hill, located in the northern suburb of Lhasa City."

"On Earth?"

He nods.

"Wait ... how?"

All in good time.

"What am I doing here?"

Cascade of gentle laughter.

The White Conch Shell is an Auspicious Symbol. It represents Knowledge and Wisdom, the first step out of your ignorance and limited consciousness. It is a wake-up call, inviting a soul toward spirituality and awakening.

I glance at the glowing tattoo. Is it imprinted on my soul?

You will spend several weeks with the debating monks, all hand clapping, loud statements and extravagant gestures. Philosophical debate is one of the paths to wisdom and freedom.

"What about my body?"

Only a few hours will pass in your dimension.

True to his word, I am left at Sera Monastery.

I cannot tell if we are physical forms or something else.

Weeks pass. My intellect is sharpened. I develop more critical thinking. An array of concepts, counter-concepts and arguments jostle in my headspace. Soon I am asking more discerning questions. I feel alive and energised.

I enquire of the lama: "All this in preparation for what?"

He does not answer. Instead a barrage of demanding thought-puzzles and strenuous cognitive challenges.

One day he simply bows before me. Bids me farewell.

Wave of his hand. I am flung through the vortex.

Returned to my body in the hotel bed.

Feel incredibly heavy. Can't move.

Blackness. Disappear into sleep.

* * *

In the morning, I wake shattered.

Exhausted. As if I am very ill.

The voice is kind and tender.

It's going to hurt for a few days.

I nod meekly.

The cost of accelerated learning.

"Any suggestions?"

Nutritious food. Infrared sauna. Massage. Walks by the ocean.

"Dark chocolate?"

At least 85% cacao.

I manage a feeble smile.

You might be interested to know that the Pleiadeans and Lyrans wore a conch shell cut at the cross-section, a memento of their Atlantean past.

"Whaaaat?"

I stare blankly.

A gentle sigh.

Did you read the book Atlantis?

"Um, no …"

It's the book before this one.

My mind is tripping. I'm really tired.

You've been breaking the fourth wall, haven't you?

I grin sheepishly.

Now I am breaking the fifth wall.

"Oh yeah?"

Yeah. Read Atlantis before you go any further.

"Alrighty then."

My eyes flutter closed.

The presence is gone.

I drift into dreamless sleep.

* * *

I spend the next few days reading on the beach.

Clearly, there is a synchronised overarching plan. A mystical series of lessons and journeys. All constructed in a way to lead to deeper understanding of life, the universe and everything.

I am only on page 42 and have a long way to go.

The noisy flapping draws my attention. Seagulls fighting for scraps. Glint in their eyes. Hint of something more.

Perhaps a higher purpose.

Repose the book on my lap and gaze awhile at the gorgeous ocean.

Life doesn't get much better than this ...

I always think it is the simple things that matter.

People are strongly influenced by all those extrinsic motivators ... stimulants and incitements flowing from outside of ourselves ... advertisements urging us to buy more, do more, be more ... magazines inspiring us toward sexier bodies, increased physical attraction ... in-vogue clothing and alluring hairstyles ... the most recent technology ...

Almost every newsfeed article is headlined '20 steps to ...' and '14 ways to ...' Yaaaawn! It's so boring.

Yet all we really need is clean air ... healthy sunshine ... pristine nature ...

And time to do nothing.

Be who we are.

Just be.

My eyelids feel lazy. Fluttering a little. Demanding a rest. Who am I to argue?

Stretch my body. Get comfortable.

I am in a small white boat surrounded by endless turquoise water … the waves are choppy … rocking to and fro … strange sensation … pervading stillness … sensing the ocean desiring to swallow me … submerge me … absorb me … adore me … love me.

Wake with a start.

Oh, just a dream.

Shake my head. Retrieve the book. Dust off the sand.

It's late. Missed the sunset.

Disappointed, I traipse back to the hotel.

Clamber into the large cosy bed.

Concede to another delicious rest.

* * *

He came in the night.

I heard the crunching of almost-black combat boots around 2:45 am.

Yeah, I know. It's pretty early … or late … depending on your point of view.

This time I was more prepared.

I was going to get answers.

Raising my hand into a 'halt' sign before the purple coat ceased flaring.

"My friend, you have not introduced yourself."

Serene smile settles upon his face.

Michael. My name is Michael.

I nod slowly.

"Yeah, but who are you?"

Are you sure you want to know?

My forehead creases impatiently.

"Absolutely."

A Keeper of the Light. Call me a maverick, if you prefer.

"Wait … what?"

A maverick is an unorthodox and independent-minded individual.

"No, the first part."

A Keeper of the Light. Did you read They Walk Among Us?

"Seriously? Are you going to tell me to read another book?"

He rolls his eyes in mock despair.

What am I going to do with you?

"Can you give me the short version?"

Sure, it's out of context, but here we go:

My home is a blissful place located near to the Source. Run by a hierarchy of powerful spiritual entities. At the top, concealed in a sacred temple, are beings that burn so bright that it is impossible to look upon them (unless they temporarily modify their energy field). These Keepers of the Light are closely connected to the Source. The administrators and rule enforcers are called Overseers. Messengers and Guardians are the teachers and guides who work in many worlds. Chasers are Messengers who have been granted special powers to rein in errant behaviour. And on the lowest rung are the Walkers. Incarnated angels. Beings who once had supreme knowledge and power but now are as limited as the humans they walk among.

Deep sigh. "Guess I need to read the book."

Indeed.

Gaze up at the ceiling. Collect my thoughts.

"Why are you here?"

You opened the magick book. You chose the Path of Light.

My mouth scrunches slightly.

"Yeah. There's that …"

Pregnant pause.

"So, what's next?"

You know what to do.

I grab the large book from the bedside table.

Admire the dark green swirling cover.

Tentatively tickle the purple stitching.

The book swiftly opens.

On the page a picture is appearing.

Jewelled parasol.

Remember, you always have free will.

I grimace with anticipation.

Place my palm upon the shimmering icon.

Searing heat! Pain shoots up my wrist.

Biting my teeth very hard.

After several minutes it subsides.

I gaze at my inner forearm.

A tattoo of a jewelled parasol.

Now each of my forearms has a tattoo.

"What is the meaning of these icons?"

The Ashtamangala are a sacred suite of Twelve Auspicious Symbols endemic to Buddhism, Hinduism and Jainism. These symbols are 'yidam' (points to focus the mind or attention) and teaching tools. Each energetic vibration reflects a position on the enlightened mindstream. As you may have noticed, each tattoo is also a gateway to a specific magick level.

"I have no idea what you are talking about."

Casual shrug.

That's what happens when you skip books in the mystical series.

"What mystical series?"

You want me to keep breaking the fifth wall?

I purse my lips. Hold my breath.

"Are we going on another journey?"

We are indeed. You ready?

The tattoo erupts into light. I see the huge colourful spinning vortex.

Trying to relax … let go … surrender …

Below, my body slumbers peacefully.

The gleaming jewelled parasol guides us along the vortex.

Ah, of course, another door.

Ominous, imposing and dark.

Spontaneous shiver.

"What's behind this door?"

Wave your tattoo. It grants access.

"Oh, yeah."

Another lama in a maroon robe and sandals.

I bow respectfully.

"Where are we?"

"Potala Palace, the former winter residence of the Dalai Lamas. The palace is named after Mount Potalaka, the mythical abode of the bodhisattva Avalokiteśvara."

"In Lhasa, Tibet?"

The lama nods kindly.

You will spend a month here. Once again, only a few hours will pass in your dimension.

"What am I here to learn?"

The Jewelled Parasol is an Auspicious Symbol. It represents Protection from dark forces, harmful forces and negative energies. Without acquiring mastery of Protection, you cannot ascend to the next level. Part 1 of the foundation is Knowledge and Wisdom, part 2 is mastery of Protection.

Michael disappears, leaving me with the lama.

The jewelled parasol, it turns out, is a spiritual-energetic protection device. The gleaming effect results from its multi-faceted gem-like quality that splits the Light into numerous colours. It is rather fascinating, and under the lama's patient tuition I learn to wield it skilfully.

Apparently, the jewelled parasol will be very useful as I walk this Path.

After a month, the lama gently pats my back and sends me spiralling down the vortex.

I arrive in my body with an inelegant whump.

Michael is standing at my bedside.

I look up at him in deep fatigue.

"Infrared saunas and chocolate?"

He nods compassionately.

Touches my shoulder.

I blink a few times.

Then sleep forever.

* * *

I have a confession to make.

Yes, I am a sofa surfer ... avid reader ... adept chillaxer ...

But, I do enjoy working out in the gym.

Exercise, like nutrition, is a very personal choice.

As always, you need to do your research, heed medical guidelines, possibly employ the services of a personal trainer, and definitely explore and discover what works best for your body.

Why do I enjoy exercise?

It promotes health and well-being. It's an investment is this earthly vehicle. It makes me feel vital and energised.

We each have our own goals: health, strength, fitness (general or fit-for-purpose), energy, muscle increase, body fat decrease, body shaping.

Here is one of the keys I have learned. Fortunately, I am naturally lazy (yep, that's a good thing), or call me energy-economical if you like. Or even better, recall the principles of Bruce Lee: functional efficiency (minimum effort with maximum results); simplicity (only keep what works); directness (not waste time); fluidity (not fixed or rigid); adaptability (flow with the situation).

How does this apply to exercise?

The question is: How often do I need to exercise, and what type of exercise can I do, that will require the least amount of energy-and-time investment while yielding maximum results (aligned with my goals)?

Let me briefly introduce a fabulous concept:

High-Intensity Interval Training (HIIT)

Long before HIIT became in vogue, Dr Ellington Darden was espousing and promoting the principles of intense infrequent training. If you read the books by Dr Joseph Mercola and Dave Asprey, you will discover the principles and benefits of HIIT. You can research it yourself. Also, a competent personal trainer will be able to tutor or supervise you.

Similar principles are used in Tabata training, developed by Japanese scientist Dr Izumi Tabata and a team of researchers from the National Institute of Fitness and Sports in Tokyo.

I also recommend the book The Anatomy of Stretching by Brad Walker. It is an excellent illustrated accompaniment to your exercise strategy.

A final thought about exercise: Find an activity you enjoy. If you don't enjoy it, you will not continue it. You will struggle with motivation. Healthy nutrition and exercise need to become a lifestyle not an episode.

Enough said. I am going to the gym for a workout.

I need to clear my mind from the sudden craziness that has become my life.

Who is this Michael anyway?

Why should I read the other books in the mystical series?

Why is this happening to me? Have I been chosen? Or did I choose this?

Is there such a thing as destiny? Or is it just intention and free will?

What is spiritual-and-emotional gravity and how does it apply to my life?

Is it all a substance-induced hallucination? Am I really travelling to Tibet?

What on earth is actually happening to me?

Aaaaarghhhh!!

The downside of being a lone ranger is no one to talk to about issues. Who could I share this intriguing weirdness with anyway?

Hence, I am going to the gym.

To work it out.

* * *

Life is a beach.

For some it is a rain forest, a national park, or lofty mountains.

I love the beach.

Sumptuous ocean views, invigorating fresh air, serene sunrises and enchanting sunsets.

I am not one to slather on sunscreen and bake in the midday sun. I adore the early mornings and late afternoons, when the temperature is optimal and ambience sensational.

Huntington Beach is a seaside city in Orange County, Southern California. Also known as 'Surf City' it flaunts a 15-kilometre long beach, mild climate and excellent surfing.

It is 10:00 am … and my toes are gently curling in the soft sand … lovely deep breaths … warm sun caressing my shoulders … relaxation permeating my body …

I sense the scrunch … Michael sits beside me … in his combat boots and long purple coat.

Makes me smile.

"Bit overdressed, aren't you?"

Insouciant shrug.

If you believe what you see.

"Hmm?"

He points across the North Pacific Ocean.

I used to surf the waves in Hawaii. It's that direction.

"I know where it is."

I lived in Kauai. The island has more sand beaches along its 177-kilometre coastline than any other Hawaiian island and surfing opportunities abound. There are wonderful waves from Haena and Hanalei on the north shore to Kealia on the east shore, Poipu on the south shore and Polihale on the west shore. Truly spectacular.

"You had a human form?"

Indeed.

"Let me guess. Another book?"

He draws in the sand. I turn my head and squint. Ah, that archaic beast.

What do you know about dragons?

I cough softly.

"Myth and speculation. Nothing more."

Michael raises his hands, palms upward.

Every sorcerer has a dragon. It is protocol.

Can't tell if he is being serious.

"What is a sorcerer?"

Extends his hand to shake mine.

I am a sorcerer. It's great to meet you.

Exude a sigh. "What is sorcery?"

Sorcery (aka magick) is practiced by a sorcerer (aka a magickian). Sorcery is the wielding of consciousness and energy to create and manifest realities, ideally in synchronisation with high-resonance beings of light and the Source.

"It's about magick and power?"

Exactly.

"Very intriguing."

It's the next step on the Path.

Shuffling uncomfortably.

"Oh."

Let me explain the different manifestations of sorcery.

"There is not one type?"

A sorcerer learns the mystical skill and art. He (or she) blends that with his temperament, disposition, knowledge and passions. He also aligns to the Light or the Dark. All that dictates the type of work he will do, and the lifestyle he will lead.

"Ok ..."

Unfortunately, there are sorcerers that align with the Dark. Of course, that is not limited to sorcerers. Many beings in diverse fields align with the Dark. That is a life choice.

Feeling a little apprehensive.

Each sorcerer finds his own expression. Some walk the path of Shamanism. Some surrender into deepest Awareness. Others immerse entirely into Love. Still others blossom into tantalising Tantrikas.

"What's next for me?"

You need to test the path of Shamanism.

"If I don't like it?"

Then simply discard it.

"How do I proceed?"

The hand points south.

You spend a few months in Mexico.

I frown morosely.

Not so keen?

Staring at the glimmering sand.

"Can I read a book instead?"

Michael bursts into laughter.

Sure. The title is The Fractal Key. Learn and absorb as much as you can.

He stands up and smiles.

See you in a few days.

I watch him stride across the sand, long purple coat flaring.

Wonder what he meant by *If you believe what you see.*

I reach for my phone and download the book.

Ah, modern technology. Easy and efficient.

There it is. Ready and waiting.

First I need a nice cosy nap.

Yawn and long stretch

Pull my cap down.

Slumber into surf.

* * *

There's something strange about the post-midnight hours. Let's name it the 2:00 - 5:00 am shift.

This is typically when exotic events occur, including vivid dreams, lucid dreams, out-of-body travels and 'alien abduction' experiences. Researchers and psychonauts speculate that those are correlated with increased DMT production in the brain (possibly the pineal gland) which occurs in the early hours of the morning.

According to the book The Fractal Key:

'DMT or dimethyltryptamine is widely distributed throughout the plant and animal kingdoms. It is a naturally occurring chemical found in mammals, marine animals, toads, frogs, mushrooms, barks, grasses, flowers and roots. DMT is molecularly similar to the fungal psychedelic psilocybin (aka magic mushrooms) and the human neurotransmitter serotonin (aka 5-hydroxytryptamine). Human brains synthesise and secrete endogenous DMT. When naturally occurring levels of DMT in the brain are raised above a certain threshold (due to events like physical death or ingestion of an entheogen) radical spiritual and psychological experiences ensue.'

Interestingly, science does not yet have sufficient answers. Consciousness and altered states are still a wonderful mystery.

You wonder why I raise this matter?

Yep, you guessed it.

It is 3:45 am. Here comes my mentor.

Thing is, I am definitely wide awake. Sipping from a glass of water.

I have to laugh. The phrase 'We're not in Kansas anymore' springs to mind. You know ... when you're way beyond your comfort zone or scope of understanding.

In my case, it's more apt to say 'We're not in Nevada anymore'. I grew up in Mesquite, which occupies the northeast corner of Clark County, about 220 kilometres from Area 51.

I greet him cordially.

"What's up, Michael?"

You ready to meet your dragon?

"Whaaaat?"

Come on. Grab the book.

I reach reluctantly for the green tome.

Deep breath. Resolute stare. Caress the ornate stitching.

The book flips open. Reveals a gorgeous blue-green dragon.

I place my palm upon the gleaming icon.

My back feels a spreading heat. Less painful than before.

Michael suggests I look in the mirror.

Wow. It's covering my entire back.

Awesome and gorgeous!

"What is the significance of the tattoo?"

The Dragon is an Auspicious Symbol. Let's go find out.

The room suddenly fills with white light. A colourful vortex opens up.

Here we go again ... spinning ... intense scchhh sound ... countless multicoloured doors ...

We halt before a large turquoise archway.

Welcome to my world.

"Your world?"

He nods.

Home.

Endless landscapes stretch before me: spectacular consortiums of dancing flowers, majestic trees, stone pathways, imposing statues and grand fountains. Truly magnificent.

Let's sit by the lotus pond.

I gaze at him curiously.

"Is this the blissful place located near to the Source?"

Indeed. You were paying attention.

"Why are we here?"

Close your eyes. Open your energy field.

"How?"

Faith and intention.

"And then?"

Invite your dragon.

The air suddenly cools. Seems like a grey mist rolling across the land.

I feel the pressure-wave of wind ... then a screech ... and finally huge blue wings come into view ... golden glow emanating from its mouth and eyes ...

"Are you sure it's friendly?"

He shrugs indifferently.

The impulse to run takes over my being.

Michael regards me sternly.

Never run from a dragon.

"What should I do?"

Stand still and do nothing.

It hovers over me. Penetrating stare into my soul.

Eternal minutes pass.

Then it lands with a muffled growl.

It likes you. Introduce yourself.

Soft sigh of relief.

I bow respectfully.

"Allen Tihkal."

Energy wafts into my consciousness.

Blaze

I look at Michael quizzically.

Yes, they are telepathic. You passed the test. You are bonded forever.

The large eyes peer at me.

What is the meaning of your name?

"Allen means 'harmony'. Tihkal is the surname my mother adopted by deed poll. She insisted my father change his surname too. It is the title of a book by Alexander (Sasha) Shulgin and Ann Shulgin called TiHKAL or 'Tryptamines I Have Known and Loved'."

*Ah, yes. Sasha ascended to our world in 2014. He was a brilliant psychedelic chemist who lived on Earth. He wrote these wise words: 'A rare and precious transcendental state, which has been called a peak experience, a religious experience, divine transformation, a state of Samadhi and many other names in other cultures. It is a state of bliss, a participation mystique, a connectedness with both the interior and exterior universes, which has come about after the ingestion of a psychedelic drug, but which is not necessarily repeatable with a

subsequent ingestion of that same drug. If a drug (or technique or process) were ever to be discovered which would consistently produce (that level of) experience in all human beings, it is conceivable that it would signal the ultimate evolution, and perhaps the end, of the human experiment.'

"Human souls ascend to this plane of existence?"

Blaze roars his displeasure.

They Walk Among Us

I groan inwardly.

Hesitate a few moments.

"What is the purpose of dragons?"

Dragons are keepers and purveyors of sacred knowledge. We are teachers to those with magick tattoos. We protect the sorcerers.

"Is that why conventional establishments tried to kill the dragons?"

Indeed.

The iridescent wings expand gracefully and he sways into the heavens.

I am alone with Michael beside the lotus pool.

Is that enough for one night?

Feel dazed and confused.

So much is happening.

"Yes. Take me back."

We jump through the shimmering vortex ... find my body curled up asleep in bed ... re-enter with a gentle thud ... everything aches ... deep fatigue ...

Ah, here comes the yummliciousness.

Rest, relaxation, recuperation.

Deep sleep.

* * *

Wake with a smile.

Daylight peeking through the curtains.

Birds tweeting and chorusing.

Nature's own alarm clock.

You're probably thinking 'Does this guy ever get out of bed?'

I assure you I do, if only to change the pillowcase.

So, I am thinking about the shamanic path.

I have read and absorbed The Fractal Key.

The book is fascinating and intriguing ... but I am not interested in living with shamans and trying 'entheogens' ... even though they can be positive and powerful and radical.

Entheogens are appropriate for spiritual adventurers and psychonauts.

I prefer a more sedate path.

What were the options again?

Awareness. Love. Tantra.

Limited menu.

Au contraire!

I jump in fright.

"Michael, can't you knock?"

On the contrary, my protégé.

"What ...?"

There are many paths to the mountaintop.

"Right ..."

You'll find yours.

"Are we going on another journey?"

If you feel ready and willing.

"Sure, let me brush my teeth."

I nip to the washroom for a few minutes, then return and plump up the pillows. May as well get the body comfortable.

Michael hands me the magick book.

Going to dive in. No point lingering.

I caress the ornate purple stitching.

The book opens. An icon appears.

A dark silver skull.

"Oooh. Shivers."

Hand down. Chest burning.

"Brilliant. Always wanted a fist-sized skull tattooed between my pectorals."

Michael looks at me peculiarly.

You want to go back to your old life?

"Um ... no."

Quit complaining.

Consider me admonished.

"What does this tattoo represent?"

The Skull is an Auspicious Symbol. It is the mark of the sorcerer. It gives access to the power and magick you seek. And it upgrades your relationship with Blaze.

"In what way?"

Dragons protect sorcerers.

"Oh yes. I remember."

Fiery flames suddenly leap from my chest.

The spinning vortex of light fills the room.

We leap in and surf the shimmering waves.

A beautiful large wooden door materialises.

To my surprise, a lama waits on the other side.

I adopt the prayer position and bow respectfully.

"Where are we today?"

He smiles benevolently.

"In Shigatse, Tibet. Tashi Lhunpo Monastery."

I bid Michael adieu and follow the monk.

After a brief tour, we repose in a huge courtyard.

Warm sun is shining ... viridescent trees shimmer in a light breeze ... contemplating the maroon walls and golden curved rooftops ... it's all rather beautiful.

The lama begins his discourse.

"As a sorcerer you need to understand the concept of 'cosmic astrology'."

I nod stoically.

"Cosmic astrology reaches far beyond the Earth plane. It includes emanations from the multi-dimensions."

I recall excerpts from The Fractal Key:

'You are surrounded by television, radio and phone signals ...

Similarly, you are surrounded and permeated with the multi-dimensions. These are not places as much as vibrations or radiances of the Light. You are swimming in multitudinous overlapping waves yet you remain unaware of their communication until you retune your innate receiver. The receiver is your consciousness. You retune it by using a catalyst or fractal key. Fractal keys open the portal to the multi-dimensions. These keys include meditation, prayer, fasting, drumming, dancing, yoga, tantra, shamanism, teacher plants, psychedelics and entheogens.'

He glances at me to ensure I am listening.

"There are many beings populating our universe: physical beings in physical worlds and radiant-energy beings in the multi-dimensions. They all have an agenda. Most serve the Light and work toward the advancement and bliss of all entities. The Universal Council of Light coordinates and orchestrates the diverse intentions and actions of the multi-dimensions."

My brow furrows. "How does this relate to me or this planet?"

Kind-hearted smile.

"Patience, young grasshopper. All will be revealed. Cosmic astrology is the influence, radiance and confluence of energies from the multi-dimensions onto your planet. This is important for personal and planetary opportunities."

"You mean … cosmic alignment?"

"Exactly … and divine timing."

"Aha."

"You need to pay attention to flux points."

"Flux points?"

He nods.

"The intersections of cosmic or radiant lines in your personal energy field and in planetary locations. Each flux point brings with it divine opportunities for positive change and transformation."

Staring at the grey paving stones.

"What is the method?"

"How did you invite your dragon?"

"Uh ... faith ... intention ... eyes closed ... energy field open ... hmm ... I need pragmatic guidance."

Hand gently touches my shoulder.

"In situations of emergency or crisis ... everything slows ... your awareness expands ... your senses are sharpened ... there's an insight, a clarity ... followed by direct and immediate beneficial action."

"True. I recall such moments."

"The secret is the breath. Exhale slowly ... allow the body to deeply relax ... open the energy field. Use your expanded awareness to listen, to seek, to locate the flux points."

"Should my eyes be open or closed?"

The lama shrugs unconcernedly.

"Whichever. If open, use a defocused gaze."

For the first time, I truly understand. Trying it out. Deep breath in ... gently exhale ... sink into marshmallowness (yep, inventing that word) ... wait a bit ... ah, there ...

"Yes, I feel it. I sense the energies around me."

"Use what you see ... hear ... feel ... to guide you."

The sun is making me narrow my eyes.

Faint outline of a being walking toward me ... resplendent vibrations ... whisper in my ear ... *"Choose the right path. Find peace and joy."*

"Wow. That was quite real."

"Interesting, eh?"

"Is that a form of advanced intuition?"

The lama claps his hands loudly.

"Grasshopper, we are all the same. Every being is 'intuitive', 'psychic', call it what you will. It is nothing more than knowledge, technique and practice, practice, practice."

I watch the trees dancing in the scattered light.

Glimmering minutes evaporate.

"Tell me more about the multi-dimensions."

"That's probably above your pay grade."

Am I not ready? Is he teasing me?

Open my palms, raise my shoulders.

"I'll take a chance. Tell me."

Devoted sigh.

"The multi-dimensions are manifestations of the Self or the Source, which is the Unmanifested Consciousness."

"Ok ..."

"There are no journeys, only the shifting of perspective and raising of resonance."

"Uh huh ..."

"Ascending is merely bringing higher consciousness from the multi-dimensions."

Nod attentively.

"The multi-dimensions are a bridge to God made of forever-steps."

"Wow. Nice one."

I remember reading this in The Fractal Key:

'From one perspective, the universe is an interconnected network of consciousness, every being linked to every other being. From another perspective, the universe consists of layers of consciousness or multi-dimensions. From a higher vantage point, you understand the universe as rays of the Sun or emanations of God or radiances of the Source. Ultimately, however, you will discover there is only one Consciousness. You are that one Consciousness.'

The lama gets to his feet.

Rolls his hand into a mudra.

The colourful vortex opens.

We surf through another doorway.

"Wait ... what ... how?"

He winks mischievously.

I surrender and follow.

"Where are we now?"

"Southwest of Shigatse, on the road to Tingri. This is Sakya Monastery, the principal monastery of the Sakyapa Sect of Tibetan Buddhism. Divided by a river, the monastery comprises the northern hillside and southern valley. As the first temple of Sakyapa with over 900 years of history, it keeps numerous historical relics, including Buddhist scriptures, thangkas and art."

"Understood."

The lama points to an engraving on a statue.

"Read it to me."

I squint at the writing.

"Is that Sanskrit? Or Tibetan?"

"It is Tibetan. Sanskrit is Indo-European. Tibetan is Sino-Tibetan. These languages come from totally different parts of the world. They're unrelated linguistically."

Alright. Store that in my trivia box.

"Expand your field to read it."

Deeply exhale … relaxing … sensing …

"Attitudes you take. Choices you make."

He raises his eyebrows.

"Very good. What is it?"

Pause for a few moments.

"A living, breathing mantra."

Hand rests lightly on my shoulder.

"Excellent, grasshopper. My work is done."

"What do you mean?"

He looks disappointed for a second.

I hesitate, then "I create my own reality … I am responsible for my life … I choose my path …"

"Yes, and …?"

"As a sorcerer-in-training, I choose this path."

"Which is …?"

"Awareness!"

Perspicacious acknowledgement.

I feel the hand thrust against my chest.

Tumbling through the vortex.

Returning to my body.

Asleep in my bed.

Fulfilment.

* * *

You know where I'm headed.

Yep, I need a beach day.

Immersion in nature.

It's a requirement for a healthy soul.

I've driven south to Laguna Beach, a seaside resort city located in southern Orange County, California. It is known for a mild year-round climate, scenic coves, environmental preservation (a dedicated greenbelt) and an artist community. The Laguna Beach coastline is protected by 12 kilometres of state marine reserve and conservation.

Absolutely perfect.

A long glorious walk is in order.

I meander for hours along the rocky outcrops and sandy bays. Breathing the fresh invigorating air, admiring the spectacular ocean views, absorbing the swoosh of the waves. This truly is the life. I am considering finding a home in this county.

Around lunchtime, I sit on a wooden bench and enjoy a sandwich. My mind casts back to Katz's Deli in New York where

I had the best pastrami (on rye) sandwich of my life. Gotta love their tag line: 'No-frills deli with theatrically cranky service serving mile-high sandwiches since 1888.'

Do you also remember the locations of your best-loved meals?

Phew. Glad it's not just me.

Best-ever (AAA Alberta) beef steak: 1888 Chop House, Fairmont Banff Springs, Alberta, Canada. Yes, I was on a snowboarding vacation. Seems 1888 was a significant year for restaurants.

Best-ever lamb chop: Karoo, South Africa. This is because of the herbs of the Karoo bushes and shrubs. Ambling among the vegetation smells like walking through a spice market.

Best-ever Greek salad: Loutro, Crete, a small island surrounded by the warm Mediterranean sea, just off the mainland of Greece. What did you expect?

Best-ever chocolate slab: Blanxart artisanal chocolate made from single-origin organic cocoa. I prefer the 91% dark chocolate slab sourced from the Congo. Smooth, healthy and delicious.

Best-ever croissant: France, of course, at any authentic boulangerie (bakery). Essential qualities: crispy exterior and melt-in-your-mouth interior; well-made crust with caramel colour; griddle mark on the base; and scents of roasted flour and butter.

I often wish I could open a restaurant and serve my favourite meals from around the world. Guess that's for another life.

For now, less sauce, more sorcerer.

I stare at the rippling ocean for a long while. Feel so relaxed and peaceful.

Hmm ... I can sense my energy field lighting up.

Employ the breath ... defocus the gaze ... stillness pervades ...

It's my dragon hailing me from another dimension.

Time for another journey.

I raise my shoulders nonchalantly.

Yeah, why not?

Reach into my backpack, extract the magick book.

Can I do this by myself?

Sure, the protective dragon is near.

Run my fingers along the stitching.

The book opens; an icon is revealed.

A white lotus flower.

Hand down. Burning sensation.

Centre of my forehead.

Oh! Seriously uncool.

Fortunately it is small.

Yet hardly discreet.

Explosion of light.

Colourful vortex.

Here I am … beside a gorgeous light-blue lake.

Maroon-clad lama approaches and waves his hand.

"Welcome."

I bow respectfully.

"My friend, you are at Yamdrok Lake (means 'Turquoise Lake') situated next to the road that runs from Lhasa to Gyantse. Yamdrok Lake is one of four holy lakes, the others being Lhamo La-tso, Namtso and Manasarovar. The lake is regarded as a source of spiritual power and protection."

Wow … pristine, sacred and beautiful …

It's moments like these you understand the phrase 'earth and sky are one'.

And at an altitude of 4,900 metres … it's a truly breathtaking view.

The lama invites me to sit by the sacrosanct water.

"The Lotus Flower is an Auspicious Symbol. It represents the path of Awareness and Awakening. With its roots in mud, and flower above the water, it signifies the raising of consciousness above attachment and desire, and the revealing of pure mind."

"I am listening."

"Have you read the iconic book I Am?"

"Um … I have not."

"Put it on your reading list."

I nod agreeably.

"**Mindfulness** is the practice of bringing the scattered mind home."

Cool tag line for a spiritual business.

"Tibetan Buddhism calls this Peacefully Remaining or Calm Abiding. It is known as *shyine* in Tibetan and *shamatha* in Sanskrit. What exactly is Calm Abiding? It is befriending, settling and dissolving all the fragmented aspects of yourself. It is total acceptance of your myriad thoughts, feelings and emotions *just as they are*. No judgement or running commentary. Simple complete acceptance."

"Tell me more."

"The key is to neither indulge nor suppress your thoughts and emotions. Instead, you quietly view them with deep compassion as they arise. Gradually there is a dissipation of thoughts and emotions, and little glimpses of pure mind."

"What is the method?"

"There is no formal technique. It is something you do anytime, anywhere. As you go about your daily life, resolve to continually *observe* and *witness* your various thoughts and emotions. If you have the time and opportunity, you can do a seated meditation once or twice per day. Again, you quietly *watch* and *notice* your disparate thoughts and emotions. Whatever arises, let it flow and let it go, without clinging or holding."

"Seems easy enough."

"It is not difficult. It is just something you *do*."

"Action based on an attitude you take, a choice you make?"

He smiles serenely.

"Ah, the living, breathing mantra."

I interlace my fingers smugly.

"Indeed."

Gazing at the azure sky. I wonder …

"Is there another practice you recommend?"

He rubs his hands gleefully.

"You will need a mirror and face mask for this exercise.

"Put on the face mask and sit or stand in front of a mirror. Start narrating the story of your life. Pour out all your thoughts, concerns, fears and emotions in a free-flowing manner. Do not permit judgement or censorship. Empty the contents of your mind. Do this for at least 20 minutes (take as long as you need).

"Then remove the mask and ask the beings of light to surround you. Say nothing and watch your face in the mirror for 5-10 minutes. Finish by placing your hands on your heart chakra while looking in the mirror, and saying to yourself 'I love you deeply. Namaste.'

"Do this practice 3 times per week for at least 3 months."

I have the urge to hug the lama.

However, it is not appropriate.

Instead, I say "That's beautiful."

Scratching my chin thoughtfully.

"What exactly is pure mind?"

He ponders for a few moments.

"It is the radiant sky that exists behind the passing clouds. It is your true nature. It is the peace and joy you seek."

Ah, juicy.

"I better practice those exercises."

He tilts his head and grins.

"And read the book I Am."

Making a mental note.

The lama ushers me to the doorway and bows goodbye.

I make the jump and find myself on the wooden bench.

There is a hint of dragon breath. I feel safe and secure.

I think that's quite enough for one day.

An amble along the coast.

A nice hot bubble bath.

And into a cosy bed.

Bonne nuit.

* * *

I wake in an irritable mood.

It's unusual for me. Perhaps I am hungry.

I order orange juice and a bagel to boost my blood sugar.

I know what I have to do.

The path of Awareness requires regular action.

At very least, the practice of mindfulness.

But what is this 'pure mind'?

What is its purpose and destination?

I sense that familiar presence ...

"Michael ... hey ..."

Allen, my protégé.

"I am ready for more learning."

Time to teach about Presence.

"Presence?"

In simple terms, consider Mindfulness as inward-directed (watching your thoughts and emotions) while Presence is outward-directed (being present in the here and now).

"Not sure I understand."

Consistent mindfulness will introduce the space between your thoughts, similar to the space between musical notes. You will begin to discover the pure mind existing behind and beyond all your thoughts.

Presence is about this moment ... here and now ... this singular reality ... this singularity. It is about bringing the attention to where you are ... by noticing what you are seeing, hearing, feeling, smelling, tasting, sensing ... here and now.

"How exactly?"

Similar to mindfulness, go about your day observing and witnessing. Avoid the I. Do not think or say 'I hear ...' or 'I notice ...' or 'I taste ...'; instead, think or say 'hearing ...' or 'noticing ...' or 'tasting ...' and so forth.

"It seems the common element to mindfulness and presence is attention."

Perhaps the appropriate word is Awareness.

"Oh ... right."

Let's talk about the past and future.

I nod attentively.

Many people live in the past and future. This is usually a way to escape the present and avoid self-responsibility. You contain the experiences of babyhood, childhood and youth, yet how can you grow and evolve if you continually access and manifest your childlike patterns? Also, if you continually dwell on past relationships (both pleasant and traumatic), how will you have space for a current relationship? Think about your clothing wardrobe and its limited space. You need to discard old useless clothes to make space for exquisite new clothes. You need to discard old useless cognitions, beliefs and behaviours to make space for magnificent new ones.

Let go the past. It has passed. It is gone. Try this exercise: Grab a specific moment in the past. Visualise it clearly in colour. Then strip all movement from that scene, so it becomes frozen. Then remove all colour, so it becomes black-and-white. Then remove all sounds, so it becomes silent. Then shrink the scene gradually to the size of a postage stamp. Finally, watch it spinning away from you, until it becomes a pinprick and disappears. Take a deep breath and be fully present.

Do not live in the future. Plan, take action, and let go. Once the planning is complete, bring the attention to here and now. What if the future arrives and it is disappointing? Then you have wasted your precious time. Every moment spent in the future is a moment lost in the present. Live in this moment. Breathe ... take delight ... relish your life!

"How does this relate to pure mind?"

The more you practice mindfulness and presence, the more you will be aware of the transient and illusory nature of everything. Nothing is permanent. Nothing stays. Nothing lasts. The only constant is pure mind, that which views the transient and illusory.

"But what is pure mind?"

Underlying ubiquitous consciousness.

"Aha."

He gestures toward the magick book.

You need a twofer.

"Huh?"

Two-for-one.

I commence the process.

Back of my neck burning. "What is it?"

An Om symbol. Perfect.

Lower tummy on fire.

I glance down. "And that?"

A treasure vase.

"Ok then ..."

The room explodes into light.

We surf through the colourful vortex.

I walk confidently through the white door.

"Wow!"

"Greetings from Rongbuk Monastery, the highest monastery in the world. Located at an altitude of 4,980 metres at the north side of Mount Everest, the monastery grants the most splendid views. Everest Base Camp (EBC) is only 8 kilometres away."

It's a simple monastery with spectacular scenery.

The lama inspects the tattoo on my neck.

He motions me to sit by the stupa.

"**Om** is an Auspicious Symbol. It is the 'cosmic sound' or 'mystical syllable' or 'affirmation of the divine'. It is the most sacred mantra in Tibetan Buddhism and Hinduism. It appears at the beginning and end of most Sanskrit mantras, prayers and texts."

I nod deferentially.

"Om contains infinite knowledge which is mysterious and inexhaustible. Om connects to the creative power of the universe. Om is the essence of everything that exists."

He draws the symbol in the sand.

"Aum and Om are precisely the same. You pronounce it Ohm. The misinformed difference between Aum and Om is simply one of transliteration, because in Sanskrit the sound O is a diphthong (blending of two vowel sounds) that is spelled AU.

"The symbol of Aum (Om) consists of three curves, a semicircle and a dot.

"The large lower curve signifies the waking state (A). The middle curve signifies the dream state (U). The upper curve signifies the state of deep sleep (M). The dot signifies the fourth state of consciousness, known as *turiya* or pure mind or infinite mind. The semicircle at the top represents *maya* (illusion) and separates the dot from the other three curves. The Aum (Om) symbol therefore represents both the manifested and unmanifested consciousness."

My head bobs appreciatively.

"It's a very cool tattoo."

I ponder the discourse for a while.

"How does this connect to awakening?"

The lama is emanating tranquillity.

"Practicing mindfulness, presence and various forms of meditation will assist you to transcend your ordinary states of consciousness and gradually arrive at pure mind or infinite consciousness."

"That is the awakening?"

"Indeed it is."

He calmly beckons me to the doorway.

I hear a muted "tshi dlk", not sure what it means, rushed through the vortex, must ask Michael about it sometime, then a golden doorway and an impressive monastery.

Can we call this the Lama Express?

Deep bow from a maroon-clad lama.

"Welcome to Palcho Monastery aka Pelkor Chode, in Gyantse."

We amble through the beautiful lines of prayer wheels at the entrance. The lama explains that the stupa on the left is the largest stupa in Tibet. A stupa (Sanskrit 'heap') is a hemispherical structure containing relics (usually the remains of Buddhist monks or nuns) that is used as a place of meditation. He tells me that *pradakhshina* (circumambulation) is an important devotional ritual in Buddhism, and stupas always have a *pradakhshina* path around them.

We walk inside the magnificent temple to the right of the stupa. As with all Tibetan monasteries and temples, you may not take photos inside. This is strictly monitored and security cameras are everywhere. The awe-inspiring interiors and towering statues within the monasteries and temples can only be stored as soulful memories.

Following his guidance, I acquire and light a butter lamp, then say a prayer for my relationships and for the whole world. He places his hand on my head and gives me a blessing. Tears inexplicably fall. No one seems to notice.

The lama leads me out to the sunny courtyard.

We sit near a tall pole covered in prayer flags.

"Are you ready for advanced lessons?"

I consent studiously.

"The Treasure Vase is an Auspicious Symbol. It represent the treasure within each person.

"Close your eyes and imagine an empty vase. The space inside the vase is exactly the same as the space outside the vase. The space is separated by the delicate walls of the vase. Pure mind or infinite consciousness is enclosed within the walls of your ordinary mind. Practicing mindfulness, presence and various forms of meditation gradually cracks the walls of the vase.

"Eventually the entire vase shatters. Then the space inside merges with the space outside. At that point, you realise you were never separate. There is only one Consciousness.

"That is the **Awakening**."

It's becoming crystal clear.

The lama continues.

"Imagine a drop of water deeply immersed in an ocean. Surrounding the drop is a fragile veneer. That veneer is the ordinary consciousness aka the ego, which is all that separates the water inside the drop from the water outside the drop. You are the drop in the ocean. When the boundary of your consciousness dissipates, you discover you are the Ocean."

"I understand."

"Most people search for the truth outside of themselves. You need to become an 'inside-er', seeking the truth within your own mind. The seeker is the sought. The search is here and now. The treasure is within you."

"Tell me more about the mind."

The lama heaves a sagacious sigh.

"Tibetans call ordinary mind *sem*. *Sem* discriminates and views reality in a dualistic way. It separates the perceiver from the perceived. It constantly relates to the 'other' and the 'world out there'. *Sem* desires, plans, strategizes, and attaches to 'external reality', with concomitant negative thoughts and emotions. It is desperately trying to prove its existence."

"Can I use the term 'ego'?"

"*Sem* or ego is a ceaselessly unsatisfied monkey jumping from branch to branch. Hence, the term 'monkey-mind' for ordinary consciousness. *Sem* is a candle flame near an open window, relentlessly exposed to the breezes of conditioning and habit."

"What about pure mind?"

"Tibetans call pure mind *rigpa* or *turiya*. *Rigpa* is pristine awareness: the radiant light of Existence, the Sky beyond the ever-moving clouds. Recall the treasure vase or the drop in the ocean. The nature of pure mind is the nature of everything."

"Underlying ubiquitous consciousness?"

"One Mind. One Consciousness."

The prospect of awakening ...

"What should I do?"

He gazes at me intently.

"Practice mindfulness and presence."

"And seated meditation?"

"Yes. I prefer the Aum / Om / I Am Meditation."

"Never heard of it."

"You heard of Stephen Shaw?"

"That mystical esoteric author?"

"Yes. Have you read his books?"

Shuffling uncomfortably.

"On my to-do list."

"Here is the **Aum / Om / I Am Meditation**.

"Start and end your day with this meditation. If you are very busy, then only do at the start of your day. Each meditation lasts 20-30 minutes, whatever time feels right for you. Sit comfortably with good posture on a meditation cushion, chair or sofa (if you need back support). You can even lay on your back on a sofa or bed with arms at either side of your body.

"Use a meditation timer with sounds that are pleasant and not disruptive. For example, download the Zazen Meditation Timer app onto your cell phone. Set the preparation phase for 1 minute then a chime/bell; set the meditation phase for 18-28 minutes (your choice) then a chime/bell; set the awaken phase for 1 minute then a chime/bell.

"Lay or sit comfortably. Start the timer. Close your eyes. During the preparation phase just relax quietly. Nothing to do. Allow any final body adjustments. The bell/chime will ring after 1 minute.

"During the meditation phase (which lasts 18-28 minutes), mentally repeat the word 'Om' (pronounced Ohm) or the words

'I Am'. Do not rush the mantra. Use a comfortable pace. *Mantra, pause, mantra, pause, mantra, pause.* Here is a key guideline: If your mind drifts into a thought, and you realise you are not repeating the mantra, simply start using the mantra again. No effort, no pressure, no performance, no judgement. Just bring yourself back to the mantra every time you become aware of having drifted away. After the allotted time, the bell/chime will ring.

"During the awaken phase, cease using the mantra, and stay seated or laying with your eyes closed. After 1 minute the final bell/chime will ring. Gradually open your eyes and return to normal wakefulness."

"Any more advice?"

"Yes. When you meditate, have no goal. Do not strive to achieve a particular state. Use a non-grasping attitude. Every meditation is different. Accept the meditation as it is. Also, be dedicated to doing regular meditation. Consistent practice is crucial."

"What kind of results should I expect?"

He raises his eyebrows.

"Non-grasping attitude, always. However, you may have more spaces, less thoughts, more responding, less reacting, more serenity and contentment, less stress and perturbation, as well as glimpses into the true nature of mind which is the true nature of everything."

"Hmm ... worth it."

"Awakening is the ultimate spiritual evolution and destination of all spiritual paths."

Noticing the shifting ambient energy.

Glance at the peaceful lama.

"You're going to shove me into the vortex, aren't you?"

He smiles and shoves me.

The last words I hear: "Tashi Delek."

Arrive back in my body. It is dark outside.

Still on the bed which is convenient.

Allen, you have returned.

"You still here?"

Amiable shrug.

"What is Tashi Delek?"

It is used as a greeting and goodbye. Tashi means 'auspicious' and Delek means 'fine' or 'well'. Tashi Delek means 'Blessings and good luck' or 'May all Auspicious Symbols be here' or …

"Or what …?"

May the Buddha Force be with you.

"Love it!"

Knew you would.

I stretch and yawn loudly.

He moves toward the door.

Fais de beaux rêves.

"Thank you."

* * *

I have a much clearer understanding ...

The path of Awareness is a delectable path. A path of action, attention, awareness, and finally awakening.

Trying to cast my mind back.

A being told me *'Choose the right path. Find peace and joy.'*

I can't remember who ...

Do I have all the components of this path?

I want to walk this path well, put some effort into it, do the job properly.

"Nothing comes from nothing," my Dad used to say. "If you want something, you have to work for it."

Even if applying functional efficiency, you still have to *do the work!*

I decide to try an experiment.

Deep exhale ... close eyes ... expand energy field.

"Michael ... Michael ... Mich –"

You called, sire?

"Sire?"

Google it.

"Thank you for responding."

He bows with a flourish.

I live to serve.

Is he being serious?

How can I help you?

"I want to acquire all the tools for this path."

Alrighty then. Where's the magick book?

I collect it from the bedside table.

He raises his hands.

You know what to do.

Tickle the stitching. Book flips open.

"Is that a Tibetan mantra?"

Put your palm onto it.

Burning my upper arm.

"That really hurts!"

Michael smiles genially.

Significant symbol.

"What does it mean?"

The Om Mani Peme Hung is an Auspicious Symbol. It represents Compassion aka Way of the Heart. It bridges the borders of the path of Awareness and the path of Love.

I scrutinise the radiant tattoo emblazoned on my arm.

Really beautiful energy emanating ...

The Indian guru Nisargadatta ascended to my world in 1981. He said: 'Love tells me I am everything. Wisdom tells me I am nothing.'

"Elucidate."

It's a summation of the perfect juncture of the path of Love and the path of Awareness.

"Right ..."

Glance at him curiously.

"Am I approaching this juncture?"

He laughs roisterously.

You are here now.

"Clarify the Way of the Heart."

Really? You need teachings about Compassion?

"Um ... it's about loving-kindness, service and generosity."

There you go. And ...?

"Forgiveness."

Uh huh ...

"Leading and inspiring with Love."

He nods sagaciously.

The Buddha is the enlightened (awakened) being. He has fulfilled the path of Awareness and path of Love. The Bodhisattva is still walking the paths ... refining his awareness ... and cultivating an attitude of bodhicitta (compassion and loving-kindness).

Gentle wave of the hand.

Room explodes into light.

Colourful vortex opens.

Light-blue doorway.

Michael introduces the being on the other side as Rinpoche (means 'precious jewel'). He explains that the title is an honorific term in the Tibetan language. It denotes a reincarnated and or highly respected and or accomplished lama.

"Where are we, Rinpoche?"

"The sacred Karola Glacier, situated alongside the road that runs from Lhasa to Gyantse. The altitude here is 5,020 metres, and the glacier top is 7,191 metres."

Wow... a multitude of prayer flags ... blues ... whites ... reds ... greens ... yellows ... tied to every viable object ... backdrop of austere ice-capped mountain ... pristine air ... a truly stupendous vista ...

We perch in front of the white-and-gold stupa.

Rinpoche smiles placidly.

"Let me expound your Auspicious Symbol. **Om Mani Peme Hung** comprises Om, the sacred syllable ... Mani, which means 'jewel' (recall the planet in 5D) ... Peme, which is the lotus flower ... and Hung, which represents the spirit of enlightenment."

"Sounds like a very special mantra."

"The sacrosanct mantra originated in India. As it moved into Tibet, the Sanskrit pronunciation changed to suit the Tibetan language.

"Here is the Sanskrit form: Om Mani Padma Hum.

"Here is the Tibetan form: Om (ohm) Mani (mahnee) Peme (pehmeh) Hung (hoong)."

I practice chanting the sacred sounds for a while.

Rinpoche gazes approvingly, then resumes his teaching.

"Om Mani Peme Hung can be chanted, spoken or thought; the written form can be viewed (e.g. on stones, objects, paper); and the written form can be engraved on spinning objects.

"Whether you chant, speak, think, view or spin the mantra, the effect is the same:

"Evocation of the spirit of compassion and awareness."

I nod enthusiastically.

"A powerful transformation tool."

His hand rests gently on my shoulder.

"What are the **2 key aspects of Love?**"

I ponder for a few moments.

Rinpoche shows his upturned palm.

"**Compassion**, which is the vital attitude and energy."

He shows his other upturned palm.

"**Loving-kindness**, which is the crucial action and doing."

He slaps his palms together, with dramatic effect.

"Neither one by itself. Both aspects are essential."

He hands me a string of colourful prayer flags.

"Hang these flags and chant the mantra."

I do as instructed. A serene blissful energy flows over me.

After twenty minutes, I sit beside him on the steps.

Rinpoche passes me a necklace of prayer beads.

"Keep these. Use them regularly."

I thank him graciously.

"Now to complete your journey … let's assimilate the mystical scents of Tibetan Buddhism …"

What does he wish to convey?

I listen attentively.

"A Prayer Wheel (aka Mani Wheel or Mantra Wheel) is a cylindrical wheel mounted on a spindle. It is composed of metal, wood, stone, leather or coarse cotton. The sacred mantra Om Mani Peme Hung or Om Mani Padme Hum is embossed or written on the outside of the wheel, often accompanied by other Auspicious Symbols. Inside the cylinder is a 'Life Tree' wrapped in multitudinous sacred mantras. A devotee spins the wheel clockwise to emanate the positive energy to all beings.

"A prayer wheel turned manually by a human being is called a stationary prayer wheel. Tibetan monasteries usually have large metal stationary wheels mounted in rows. A prayer wheel turned by flowing water is called a water wheel. A prayer wheel turned by heat of a candle is called a fire wheel. A prayer wheel turned by wind is called a wind wheel."

"Very interesting."

"A Prayer Flag has a similar purpose. Tibetans do not pray to gods. Our sacred items are used to emanate positive energy into every dimension. Hanging prayer flags in high places allows the wind to carry the prayers, mantras and blessings to all beings.

"Horizontal prayer flags (called Lung ta, means 'wind horse') are square or rectangular, and hung horizontally on string or rope between two objects in high places, e.g. monasteries, temples, stupas and mountain passes.

"Vertical prayer flags (called Darchog, means 'flagpole') are large single rectangles attached along their vertical edge to poles, e.g. in the ground, on rooftops, cairns and mountains.

"Prayer flags are traditionally arranged from left to right as blue, white, red, green and yellow. These colours represent the five elements and Five Pure Lights (blue for aether or space; white for air; red for fire; green for water; and yellow for earth)."

"Intriguing facts."

"Prayer Beads or malas (means 'garland') are used to mark the repetitions of prayers, mantras, devotions or prostrations. In Tibetan Buddhism malas are 108 beads: 100 *awareness mantras* and 8 *compassion mantras*. Some devotees use malas of 27 beads for doing prostrations.

"Prayer beads are made from Bodhi seeds (*Ficus religiosa*, the sacred Bodhi tree) or from Lotus seeds (*Nelumbo nucifera*, the sacred Lotus plant) or from Rudraksha seeds (*Elaeocarpus ganitrus*, the sacred Rudraksha tree; Rudraksha means 'Shiva's tears'). Other materials are sometimes used, e.g. carnelian, amethyst or sandalwood."

I glance down at my necklace.

Rinpoche gestures benignly.

"Those are Bodhi seeds."

As my thumb touches the first bead, I feel the soft pat on my back.

I manage to utter "Tashi Delek" as the vortex engulfs me.

Returned to the spacious hotel room.

Michael sits on the edge of the bed.

Back so soon?

"Seems so ..."

Did you acquire all you need?

Staring at the faux tracery ceiling.

"Um ... I would like to cover all the angles ... leave no pebble unturned ..."

Ah, one more destination for you.

He brings over the magick book.

I wearily touch the stitching.

Pages whirl ... icon appears.

The helm ... a ship's wheel?

Place my palm upon it.

Burns my lower back.

The Wheel of the Law.

"Which means?"

The Wheel of the Law is an Auspicious Symbol. Also known as Dharmachakra or Wheel of the Dharma, it represents the teachings of Gautama Buddha and the path to Nirvana. It is thus connected to the Four Noble Truths and the Eightfold Path. The Buddha set the Dharmachakra in motion when he delivered his first sermon.

"Awesome! I love it."

Explosion of light fills the room.

The colourful vortex tantalises me.

Beautiful ornate wooden doorway.

An illumined lama waiting on a Tibetan street.

We exchange the Tashi Delek greeting.

"Welcome to the Barkhor, or holy path of transformation. Also the site of Lhasa's bustling marketplace, the Barkhor comprises the streets surrounding and leading to Jokhang Temple, which is considered Tibet's most sacred temple."

We meander along the holy pathway, pausing only to admire a resplendent thangka (Tibetan painting on cotton or silk appliqué that depicts a Buddhist deity, scene or mandala).

I find myself immersed in a supremely peaceful ambience: devotees flicking prayer beads and muttering mantras; pilgrims rotating hand-held mani wheels; horizontal prayer flags fluttering in a celestial breeze amid engaging architecture; and, finally, vertical prayer flags draped from five 20-metre-high poles encircling the temple.

Numerous pilgrims are prostrating outside the 'house of the Buddha' (Jokhang temple). We step heedfully through the devoted throng and make our way inside the sacrosanct building. The energy is mystical and divine. As always, no photos are allowed. I diligently attempt to store every precious moment in my memory vault. After the sacred tour, we stand for a while in the open courtyard. I watch a monk serenely filling a water container from the ornate pump.

I feel the familiar hand on my shoulder.

"Wait ... before you dismiss me ... no lecture?"

A tranquil smile adorns his face.

"The energy is the lecture. The thangka is your soul."

"Whoa. That's deeper than the ocean."

Thrust through the colourful vortex.

Into my body waiting on the bed.

Groggy gaze across the room.

Ah, the protégé returns.

My words slur slightly.

"You still here?"

What now, lonely wanderer?

Shrug and purse my lips.

Something new is coming.

Stare at him curiously.

A spiritual transition.

Subtle echo in my consciousness ... remembering an ethereal message ... oh, yeah ... *'Choose the right path. Find peace and joy.'*

Michael nods astutely.

Take a few weeks. Absorb the teachings. Practice the exercises. Contemplate everything.

"Where shall I ponder?"

In San Diego.

A beach is calling me.

One more thing.

"Yes?"

Read the book 5D.

My eyes flutter sleepily.

Ripple of a gull's wing.

Warm sun caresses my face.

Swoosh of the ocean engulfs me.

* * *

San Diego is spectacular.

However, let me backtrack a little ...

Southern California (colloquially known as SoCal) is a geographic and cultural region consisting of California's 10 southernmost counties: San Luis Obispo, Kern, San Bernardino, Santa Barbara, Ventura, Los Angeles, Orange, Riverside, San Diego and Imperial. Southern California is delineated by the county lines at 35° 47' 28" north latitude, which form the northern borders of San Luis Obispo, Kern and San Bernardino counties.

Southern California exhibits a range of climates, from Mediterranean through semi-arid to desert. The weather is mostly sunny with sporadic rain.

Los Angeles County is the most populous (approximately 10 million people) county in the United States. It is also one of the most ethnically diverse counties. San Diego County is the fifth most populous (approximately 3.4 million people) county in the United States.

Here comes the juicy part:

San Diego County has more than 110 kilometres of coastline.

Yummy beaches cascade from the north ... San Onofre ... Oceanside ... Carlsbad ... Leucadia ... Encinitas ... Cardiff ... Solana ... Del Mar ... Torrey Pines ... La Jolla ... Pacific ... Mission ... Ocean ... Point Loma ... Coronado ... Imperial.

That's just ridiculous!

Where do I commence?

I decide to skip San Onofre. Although it features legendary surf spots (Trestles and Old Man's), it is also home to a decommissioned nuclear generating station. Not really my style.

Oceanside is the obvious choice. It offers wide sandy beaches, a meandering boardwalk and one of the longest (592 metres) wooden piers on the west coast. There is also a surf museum which I am keen to visit.

Soon I am nestled on a gorgeous beach, toes curling contentedly in golden sand. A soft breeze is wafting across my relaxed body. Book in hand, I get down to some serious reading.

Honestly, this is the life.

How can it get better than this?

I hear the scrunch of footsteps to my right.

A woman is unfurling a psychedelic towel.

I nod amiably. She proffers a smile.

Long blonde curly hair. Green eyes.

Focus my attention onto the book.

A few minutes later, I hear:

"Are you reading 5D?"

My eyebrows raise.

"I am. You know it?"

"Of course. It's the first book in a mystical trilogy. 5D is metaphysically deep. The sequels Star Child and The Tribe continue the mysticism while introducing the topic of Tantra."

Close an eye and gaze at the sky.

I vaguely recall the aspects of a sorcerer's path.

Awareness. Love. Tantra.

Yes, that's it.

I have journeyed down the path of Awareness and am currently bridging onto Love. Not really sure about Tantra.

My pondering may be appearing impolite.

I turn my body toward the woman.

She is wearing a one-piece aquamarine swimsuit with white sparkles. Exuding a confident yet gentle energy. I feel relaxed and comfortable in her presence.

"Hi, my name is Allen Tihkal. Bibliophile, book collector, globetrotter, chillaxer and contemplator."

She giggles softly.

"That's quite a mouthful, Mr Tikhal. How shall I counter?"

Protracted pause.

"I am Sarita de Beauvoir. Tantra master, artist, gastronome and world traveller."

"Wow, your bio is much sexier than mine."

She stares at me coldly.

"Uh, no, I meant the words, the self-description."

Sarita bursts into laughter.

"Just playing with you, Allen. I know what you meant."

My cheeks are blushing slightly.

I blurt "Judging a woman by her face or body is abhorrent. The imposed assessment criteria from magazines, culture and advertising is disgusting."

She nods agreeably.

"All that counts is the heart and soul."

I feel the ripples of tender energy.

She rises to give me a side-on hug.

"Absolutely, Allen."

We chat for a long while. The intense, slightly awkward beginning moves into a pleasant, engaging dialogue. She is an intelligent woman with a lovely personality. And I do like intelligence.

At my invitation, she pulls her towel closer to mine.

We settle into our books. The ambience becomes still and cosy. I notice she is reading We Should All Be Feminists by Chimamanda Ngozi Adichie. How interesting.

Later, as the sun disappears over the horizon, we say our goodbyes.

I have been single forever (by choice, I'll have you know) but I don't want this opportunity to slip by me.

My hesitant voice warbles in the cooling air.

"Can we meet again?"

She nods cheerfully.

"Nominate a beach. I'll be there."

Thinking quickly.

"Uh … Moonlight Beach, Encinitas … in two days?"

"3:00 pm … I'll have a picnic basket."

"Fantastic. See you then."

She bows a "Namaste".

(Namaste is spoken with a slight bow and palms pressed together, fingers pointing upward, thumbs close to the heart chakra. Namah means 'bow' or 'reverential salutation' and te means 'to you'. Spiritually, it conveys the notion 'the divine in me and you is the same' and therefore signifies 'the divine in me bows to the divine in you'.)

I return a "Namaste", and watch her walk serenely away.

* * *

San Diego, you are so cool!

Yes, I arrived early (it's a habit) and surveyed the area.

Encinitas is a delightful fusion of '60s-inspired beach culture with boutique shopping, contemporary restaurants, meditation gardens and yoga studios.

Moonlight Beach flows south toward Swami's Beach. Swami's Point is a popular surf spot (right point break) located below the golden-spired Encinitas Temple. The temple is a branch of Self-Realization Fellowship (SRF), an international organisation founded by Paramahansa Yogananda to disseminate the teachings of Kriya Yoga.

And right on time … the lovely vision of Sarita strolling toward me.

Wicker picnic basket in hand … towel draped over her shoulder.

What is rumbling more … my heart or tummy?

A brief hug and affectionate greeting.

Feel a moment of wariness within me.

'Proceed with caution. Don't get hurt.'

From where did that arise?

We are soon chatting about life … the universe … and everything.

The blanket flaunts gastronomical yumminess:

Carne asada burritos, featuring thinly sliced strips of seasoned steak, shredded cheddar cheese, cotija cheese, crema and guacamole. The guacamole, she explains, is made with green mango, chile de árbol, tomato, pomegranate and candied walnuts.

Palate cleanser of sumptuous pureed strawberries, raspberries and blueberries.

Dessert is cocoa-infused tiramisu pancakes with drizzles of espresso syrup, and mounds of mascarpone and cocoa whipped cream.

I think my taste buds are having an orgasm.

Familiar sweet giggle.

"The ultimate slacker-surfer lunch."

"It was fabulous. Thank you."

"You're welcome."

Tummies purring contentedly in the late afternoon sun. Refreshing ocean breeze. Gorgeous blue ocean extending before us. It's kinda purrfect.

"Sarita, I'd love to hear about Tantra."

She stretches lazily and yawns.

"After my nap, ok?"

"Hey, no worries."

Soft laughter.

"Just kidding. You ready?"

Tilt my head attentively.

She glances at the shimmering sand.

"First, let's clear up a vexing myth:

"Tantra is not all about sex."

I feign disappointment.

"The teachings derive from the ancient Vigyan Bhairav Tantra, a scripture reputed to be at least 5,000 years old, which is written as a conversation between Lord Shiva and his consort Shakti. Tantra merges deep meditation, emotional fluidity and sexual openness."

"Sounds boring ..."

She slaps my shoulder, then resumes.

"Tantra is a journey within your seven chakras. It is also connecting to the chakras of your romantic partner. Together you walk the path to the Light."

"Uh huh ..."

"Tantra is a love story. It is exquisilicious existence."

I shuffle uncomfortably.

Penetrative stare.

"Unpleasant memory?"

I feel a tear well in my eye.

Clearing my throat.

"I have not had a relationship in a while."

"Tell me what happened."

"Can I use a metaphor?"

"Sure."

"A man walks from his apartment to the office every morning. It is only a few blocks, and probably takes him about 15-20 minutes. He follows the same route, invariably encountering an angry homeless person. His guilt and love prompt an array of actions: food, money, advice, and even hugs. Almost every day the homeless person slaps the man's face.

"As time goes by, the man contemplates the violence. For a few months, he determines that the universe must be sending him a lesson. Later, he decides he must have bad karma. Still later, he resolves to sink deeper into Love. Yet, the painful slaps do not cease.

"One day the man changes his route."

She nods sagely.

"Is that why you have been single for so long?"

"Yep ..."

"There is a time to stay and a time to exit. Wisdom is knowing the difference."

Her hand slides onto mine.

"Are you ready to move on?"

Michael's words flit across my consciousness: *'Also, if you continually dwell on past relationships (both pleasant and traumatic), how will you have space for a current relationship? Think about your clothing wardrobe and its limited space. You need to discard old useless clothes to make space for exquisite new clothes. You need to discard old useless cognitions, beliefs and behaviours to make space for magnificent new ones.'*

"Yeah, I guess I am."

Soothing loving energy flows toward me.

"In the mood for a relevant Tantric insight?"

"Go on then ..."

"The past is a graveyard of rotting corpses."

"Eeeww."

"Why revisit it? Why the attachment?"

Ignorant shrug.

"Acknowledge the pain, release the emotions, then forgive and let go."

Biting my lip sanguinely.

"There is nothing more important than being *here now* in a relationship. *Presence* is the secret key to fulfilment in Tantra.

"Each moment in life is a branch point. Inhabit the *here now* fully, and the next moment is profoundly shaped by your presence and mindfulness.

"Tantra teaches us to be responsive not reactive. There is a crucial difference.

"*Reactions* stem from the *past*, arising as old thoughts, dysfunctional beliefs and harmful behaviours. If you react out of old habits, then you are not responding.

"*Responses* stem from being *here now*. From being totally alive in the moment. It is a flowing aliveness, a response to what *is*. People rarely respond; they mostly react; whenever you respond, something magical occurs."

My eyebrows raise appreciatively.

"The past does not define your identity; the past does not determine your thoughts and actions; the past does not dictate your future."

"Wow. That's awesome."

She smiles broadly.

"It's Tantra, baby!"

Sarita playfully tugs my hand, and runs toward the ocean.

I chase after her.

Oh my ... a large dragon tattoo is peeping from her swimsuit.

"Hey, wait, wait!"

Catch her in the shallow water.

"Your tattoo ... what does it mean?"

She winks coyly.

"I am a sorcerer."

Flurry of foam, raucous splash, disappears into a wave.

I am left standing, mouth agape.

* * *

The break is good for me.

Much to process and ponder.

I am sitting in my hotel room with a cappuccino.

Yes, I know. I just need one.

Thinking of consulting the magick book.

This path of Love is getting really deep.

Love is all-encompassing, all-embracing.

Tantra is a shared journey between lovers.

Tantra is therefore a microcosm of Love.

Tantra is Love's training ground.

It is easy to 'love All That Is'.

However, getting into the ring romantically, walking that path together ... that's the real deal ... in-your-face ... challenging ... evolving ... it's the crucible of Love.

(Crucible means 'a container in which metals or other substances may be melted or subjected to very high temperatures; a situation in which people or things are severely tested, often interacting to produce something new' according to the Oxford Concise English Dictionary.)

Reach for the magick book.

Come on, let's do it.

Tickle the stitching. Boom.

A glowing icon appears.

Two golden fish.

Intriguing.

Palm down.

Burning my left thigh.

Explosion of white light.

Here comes the bright vortex.

A wooden maroon doorway.

An old lama with a joyful face.

I follow him along an entrance walkway. It is sacred, peaceful and inspiring. The rock face bears numerous mystical inscriptions. As we approach the temple, I notice the outside walls are covered in holy paintings, and pilgrims are prostrating devotedly.

He leads me inside the sacrosanct 'lama's cave', a solitary space dedicated to prayers, mantras and blessings. The rock walls are bedecked with brightly coloured Buddhist statues and murals. Pilgrims meet the lama by making an appointment.

He bows affably.

"I am known as Sorcerer of the Heart. I don't care for titles, but sometimes they are necessary."

Returning a reverential bow.

"Where are we?"

"Sanggye Dhungu Temple, Lhasa."

"Aha."

"You are wondering about your sacred tattoo?"

"Indeed."

"Two Golden Fish is an Auspicious Symbol. It represents the intertwined path of Love, designated as Tantra. You will notice the fish are facing each other (head and tail), yet they do not touch.

"As Kahlil Gibran wrote in his book The Prophet: '... let there be spaces in your togetherness, and let the winds of the heavens dance between you ... and stand together yet not too near together: For the pillars of the temple stand apart, and the oak tree and the cypress grow not in each other's shadow.'

"Finally, the fish are immersed in the ocean. The ocean (or any large body of water) represents the Source, the Divine, the Ultimate. The Ocean of Love and Light."

I am filled with excitement and trepidation.

He scrutinises my expression.

"You need to access your individual realm."

"My ... um, what?"

"Do you know yourself?"

I shrug naively.

Devoted sigh.

"All that you believe you are has come from external sources. Your identity has been built by a relentless mind-bending stream, starting with parents, schools and friends and concreted by society, culture, media and advertising.

"Most of what you know about yourself is the opinion of others. They sing 'you are wonderful' so you believe you are wonderful. They cry 'you are ugly' so you believe you are ugly. They sing 'you are kind' so you believe you are kind. They cry 'you are bad' so you believe you are bad. And the singing and crying never ceases.

"You sculpt your identity based on multitudinous never-ending external messages.

"Of course, those are utterly meaningless. You are just you. A flower dancing in a breeze.

"You need to step away from the external mind-stream. Be alone. Acquire self-insight."

Stroking my chin thoughtfully.

"Does meditation assist this process?"

"Mindfulness is an essential practice. The I Am (or Om) meditation is important."

He gently touches my ears.

"Listen to me very carefully.

"The first step is *knowing yourself*.

"The second step is *accepting yourself*.

"If you wait for someone else to accept or endorse you (e.g. parent, sibling, friend, teacher, therapist, authority figure, fashion magazine, celebrity show, romantic partner) then you will always be *held hostage* to someone outside you!

"And what if such a person endorses you, then later disapproves of you? Your self-esteem and self-identity plummet. You are living at the mercy of wolves.

"Equally, if you seek approval from a romantic partner, then you are doomed, and your relationship is doomed."

I am shaking my head.

"Wow, that's radical."

He emphatically slaps the back of one hand onto the palm of his other hand.

"You must bring your pre-approved self to the relationship. Total self-acceptance. Just as you are. A flower dancing uniquely in a breeze.

"You are doing the work. You are mindful. You are meditating. You are peeling back the layers, discarding judgement, and accepting and embracing all you encounter.

"All layers merging into pure Love."

He waves his hands ardently.

"Do not seek happiness from those you love. Happiness does not come from outside you. Happiness does not come from other people. Happiness does not come from your romantic partner.

"You should be capable of being alone and blissful. Then your love is *no longer a need but a sharing*. A sharing relationship is divine and exquisilicious."

"Wow ... wow ... wow!"

I want to hug him, but I know the rules.

"That is brilliant! Who are you?"

He smiles with amusement.

"Sorcerer of the Heart."

"Can you recommend a practice?"

Heart Chakra Meditation. Do once a day (or as often as required) for 15-30 minutes.

"First half of the meditation: Sit or lay comfortably. Place your palms on your heart chakra. Command or request that Love energy flows from the Source into your heart chakra. Receive this energy.

"Second half of the meditation: Place your arms by your sides. Allow the Love energy to spread from your heart chakra into all your other chakras *while mentally repeating or saying this mantra* 'I love myself. I accept myself.'"

I notice the shifting resonance.

"Any closing words?"

"A few ...

"Never listen to anyone who is telling who you are. Always listen to your inner voice.

"People are keen to control you, to change you, to manipulate you, to guide you. However, the only true guide exists within you.

"Ignore imposed rules, requirements, frames, stories and ideologies.

"Be yourself. Be real. Be free."

Regarding him admiringly.

Feel the swift slap on my back.

Hear a resounding "Boomshakalaka!"

Hurtling through the vortex, I have to smile.

That crazy joyful brilliant sorcerer.

I know I'll see him again.

* * *

It's been a week since our last rendezvous.

Early days ... but I am missing her already.

We have arranged to meet at La Jolla Shores.

Yeah ... we both adore oceans.

It's a morning date. Earlier I located a scrumptious coffee shop and filled a large flask with four cappuccinos, and purchased a few croissants and pain au raisins. Hope they will satisfy her discerning French palate.

I am doing my usual reconnaissance.

Find a place on the long crescent of golden sand ... unfurl the large picnic blanket ... drop my beach bag ... leave my towel rolled at one side ...

Ah … here she comes.

I give her a big hug.

"Hey …"

"Hey, Allen."

"I got us some breakfast."

Reposing on the soft blanket … ocean swoosh enveloping us … twittering of birds in the distance … refreshing breeze wafting across our faces …

It's all so calm and serene.

Gazing at the cobalt water … small frothy waves racing to the shore … morning sun glinting and gleefully beckoning us …

In the sky … a vague outline … sense the unusual energy …

It's my dragon from a higher dimension.

Faint whisper.

End of the lone ranger … beginning of the path of true deep surrendered Love.

"Wonderful!" I hear Sarita exclaim.

Turn my head toward her.

"Did you hear that too?"

She smiles sweetly.

Points to another patch of sky.

I narrow my eyes.

"Expand your energy field."

Ah … right … a second dragon.

"Is it yours?"

Heartfelt accord.

"We are bonded as equals. Neither serves the other."

Quietness settles upon us once more.

Thoughts flutter across my mind.

I cough softly, then "Sarita?"

"Hmm …?"

"Your dragon's name?"

"Glow."

"Sounds Tantric."

"As in 'glows with pleasure'?"

"Yeah …"

"Yours?"

"Blaze. A fiery name."

She yawns insouciantly, then lays on her tummy.

"Please unfasten my bikini top."

"Alright … doing now …"

"If you stroke my back, I will share more about Tantra."

"I accept your tantalising deal."

Soon she is a purring kitten in a sunbeam.

After a few minutes, her lecture commences.

"There are **4 key aspects of Tantra:**

"**Acceptance**

"**Openness**

"**Intimacy**

"**Energy**"

My interest is piqued.

I am listening attentively.

"Let's start with **Acceptance**

"Acceptance is called self-love

"Acceptance is inward-directed

"Acceptance is saying 'I am OK'

"In Tantric terms, simply '**I Am**'"

Briefly recalling the words of Sorcerer of the Heart: 'You must bring your pre-approved self to the relationship. Total self-acceptance. Just as you are. A flower dancing uniquely in a breeze.'

Sarita takes a deep breath, then resumes.

"Society does not support self-love. A romantic partner or family member can often be very critical. Many people vociferate that self-love is selfish or narcissistic. And you are bombarded by negative social media and judgemental advertising.

"Practicing self-love is like a salmon struggling to swim upstream.

"However, Tantra requires that you accept yourself completely.

"If you cannot accept yourself completely, how will somebody else accept you?

"If you cannot accept yourself completely, how will you progress to Openness and Intimacy?"

Her fingertips delicately caress her temples.

"Remember when you were a young child. Standing in front of a mirror or playing in a garden. You were natural and free and self-loving. There was no judgement or self-condemnation. You simply loved and accepted yourself.

"You need to accept the entire you, exactly as you are, not as you 'should be'.

"This is the beauty of is-ness and splendour of I Am."

I slowly remove my hand from her back.

"That's truly inspiring, Sarita. Can we be children and frolic in the surf?"

She jumps up, leaving her top on the blanket.

"Fabulous idea. See you in the water!"

Here I am again, chasing a Tantrika.

Her dragon tattoo is magnificent.

Catch up to her in the shallows.

Together we go for a long swim.

I love her Atlantean energy.

Eventually we pad up the beach.

Grab our towels and dry off.

Relaxing elatedly on the blanket.

"Hmm ... I need a pain au raisin ... and a sip of cappuccino ..."

"And me ... recharge and recuperate ..."

After half an hour, I casually ask if she will continue the lecture.

"Of course. Where's your delicious hand?"

I resume stroking her back tenderly.

"There are 4 key aspects of Tantra:

"Acceptance

"Openness

"Intimacy

"Energy"

"I remember ..."

"Let's discuss **Openness**

"Openness is authenticity

"Openness is outward-directed

"Openness is saying 'I show freely'

"In Tantric terms, simply '**I Show**'"

Cupping my chin thoughtfully.

"Clearly, these are sequential stages. So ... is acceptance connected to openness?"

"Indeed, it is. If you cannot fully accept yourself, you will fear showing yourself to others. And how can intimacy develop when you are hiding parts of yourself?

"Are you ready for a succulent secret?

"Every human being is ordinary ... every human being has 'weaknesses' ... every human being is fragile ... and life is a delicate thread that can unravel at any moment.

"What, therefore, is the point of facades and egos? Only to protect deeply felt fragility.

"Such protection, however, is an illusion.

"Instead, accept your ordinariness.

"Accept your 'weaknesses'.

"Accept your fragility.

"Accept your fears.

"Only then will you truly understand that every human being is beautiful just as they are.

"We are all gorgeous, delectable and divine.

"Drop the mic. Boom."

I pretend to be alarmed. "No, no, don't drop the mic. Please continue."

She heaves a mock sigh.

"Allllllright …

"Here come the **Tantra mantras**

"Be innocent

"Be here now

"Be real. Be free

"Be spontaneous

"Be where you are at

"Be simple and unpretentious

"Be whoever you are all the time"

I clap my hands cheerfully. "Oh yeah. Say more."

"Do not use masks

"Show your real face

"Shine your light fearlessly

"Respect your thoughts and feelings

"Express yourself honestly and authentically

"Live in the present moment

"Respond instead of reacting

"Do no harm and accept no harm"

Screeeech of mental tires. "Whoa! Explain how that last one fits."

She glances up at me curiously.

"Regarding 'do no harm', there is no need to be tactless or rude. We are all walking this challenging path of life together. Respect is an essential part of the journey.

"As for 'accept no harm', the same applies. You deserve to be treated with respect. There is no reason to tolerate harsh or violent communication."

I nod agreeably.

"One final guideline ...

"Tantra requires your soul to be an open book.

"However, you need to consider the notion of boundaries.

"We live in a world that is not entirely free. Your community may have codes. Your work situation may have protocols. Your society and culture may have enforced parameters. Thus, your expression needs to be carefully tailored and adaptable.

"Also, you need to set your own personal and professional boundaries. What are your codes, protocols and tolerance points?

"Therefore, you will live as an open book, with a few pages kept hidden and sacred. You do not simply reveal everything to all people."

I am staring at the azure sky.

"Tantra seems to apply to all relationships, including broader societal ones. Yet, it is primarily focused on the romantic and spiritual intertwining of two souls. With that in mind, can I reveal all of myself to you? Can I be a completely open book with you?"

She grabs my hand passionately.

"I'd like that very much, Allen."

Sensing the shifting ambience.

I reach down and kiss her.

And everything changes.

* * *

Wowsers!

Are you feeling what I'm feeling?

There's a lot of yumminess happening.

We are apart for a few days, which is useful.

I need to process and integrate everything ... the teachings ... the new love ... the soul connection ...

My world is shifting ...

My mind is waking ...

My heart is opening ...

My soul is expanding ...

Should I consult the magick book?

Seems I can learn a lot from my Tantrika.

I am pondering my progress and path.

How many tattoos are imprinted on my body?

When I have all twelve, do I graduate as a sorcerer?

Scanning the varicoloured designs on my skin.

Michael's words rush into my consciousness: *'The Ashtamangala are a sacred suite of Twelve Auspicious Symbols endemic to Buddhism, Hinduism and Jainism. These symbols are 'yidam' (points to focus the mind or attention) and teaching tools. Each energetic vibration reflects a position on the enlightened mindstream. As you may have noticed, each tattoo is also a gateway to a specific magick level.'*

Glance at my inner forearms:

The White Conch Shell is an Auspicious Symbol. It represents Knowledge and Wisdom, the first step out of your ignorance and limited consciousness. It is a wake-up call, inviting a soul toward spirituality and awakening.

The Jewelled Parasol is an Auspicious Symbol. It represents Protection from dark forces, harmful forces and negative energies. Without acquiring mastery of Protection, you cannot ascend to the next level. Part 1 of the foundation is Knowledge and Wisdom, part 2 is mastery of Protection.

Peruse my upper back in the mirror:

The Dragon is an Auspicious Symbol. Dragons are keepers and purveyors of sacred knowledge. They are teachers to those with magick tattoos. They protect the sorcerers.

Scrutinise my chest:

The Skull is an Auspicious Symbol. It is the mark of a sorcerer. It gives access to the power and magick you seek. And it upgrades your relationship with your dragon.

Centre of my forehead:

The Lotus Flower is an Auspicious Symbol. It represents the path of Awareness and Awakening. With its roots in mud, and flower above the water, it signifies the raising of consciousness above attachment and desire, and the revealing of pure mind.

Back of my neck:

Om is an Auspicious Symbol. It is the 'cosmic sound' or 'mystical syllable' or 'affirmation of the divine'. It is the most sacred mantra in Tibetan Buddhism and Hinduism. Om contains infinite knowledge which is mysterious and inexhaustible. Om connects to the creative power of the universe. Om is the essence of everything that exists.

My lower tummy:

The Treasure Vase is an Auspicious Symbol. It represent the treasure within each person. Pure mind or infinite consciousness is enclosed within the vase of your ordinary mind. Eventually the vase shatters. You realise there is only one Consciousness. That is the Awakening.

My upper arm:

The Om Mani Peme Hung is an Auspicious Symbol. It represents Compassion aka Way of the Heart. It bridges the borders of the path of Awareness and the path of Love.

My lower back:

The Wheel of the Law is an Auspicious Symbol. Also known as Dharmachakra or Wheel of the Dharma, it represents the teachings of Gautama Buddha and the path to Nirvana. It is thus connected to the Four Noble Truths and the Eightfold Path.

My left thigh:

Two Golden Fish is an Auspicious Symbol. It represents the intertwined path of Love, designated as Tantra. You will notice the fish are facing each other (head and tail), yet they do not touch. They are immersed in the ocean, which represents the Source, the Divine, the Ultimate.

That's a lot of tattoos.

Over a lot of skin space.

I think Mom would be pleased.

She always said "Travel. Explore. Be free."

As for Dad, I am not so sure.

He used to say: "Be sensible. Take responsibility."

Hmm ... ten Auspicious Symbols ... two pending tattoos.

I wonder what is going to happen next?

Closing my eyes ... few deep breaths ...

It's time for a snooze methinks.

Tomorrow is another day.

* * *

Sarita told me about an amazing hotel in San Diego.

Hotel del Coronado (aka The Del) is a beachfront hotel in the city of Coronado, just across the San Diego Bay. The hotel is the second largest wooden structure in the United States. It was designated a California Historic Landmark in 1970 and National Historic Landmark in 1977.

The hotel opened in 1888 (there's that magic date) as the largest resort hotel in the world. It has accommodated presidents, royalty and celebrities; and been featured in numerous movies and books.

Presidents have included: Benjamin Harrison, William McKinley, William Howard Taft, Woodrow Wilson, Franklin D Roosevelt, Dwight D Eisenhower, John F Kennedy, Lyndon B Johnson, Richard Nixon, Gerald Ford, Jimmy Carter, Ronald Reagan, George H W Bush, Bill Clinton, George W Bush and Barack Obama.

Famous guests have included: Thomas Edison, Lyman Baum, Charlie Chaplin, Babe Ruth, Bette Davis, Katharine Hepburn, Barbra Streisand, Kevin Costner, George Harrison, Keanu Reeves, Brad Pitt, Madonna and Oprah Winfrey.

It seems like a wonderful opportunity to spoil myself.

As I follow the walkway in the hotel grounds, I notice a huge tree. There's a plaque just beneath the tree. It reads:

Hotel del Coronado
Dragon Tree
Dracaena Draco
Native to the Canary Islands, this unusual tree was planted
at The Del prior to the turn of the century where it thrives
in our temperate southern California coastal climate.
The dragon tree was used as a backdrop in the
Marilyn Monroe movie Some Like It Hot,
which was filmed at The Del in 1958.

Checking in at reception, I am offered more information: Dracaena is a genus of about 120 species of trees and succulent shrubs; the word derives from the Ancient Greek drakaina which means 'female dragon'. Dracaena plants (presumably the smaller versions) are suitable as houseplants, and were nominated as a top performer in NASA's clean air study.

Another interesting snippet: The hotel's original landscaping was done by Kate Sessions, the pioneer horticulturist also known as the 'Mother of Balboa Park'.

Anyway, I'm taking the dragon tree as a sign.

This is where I am meant to be.

For a few days, at least.

I am meeting Sarita this evening on Coronado Central Beach which runs along Ocean Boulevard, just north of Hotel del Coronado. It has been consistently voted one of America's finest beaches. Its unique selling point? A wide beach that literally sparkles, due to the mineral mica in its golden sand. It will probably be spectacular at sunset.

After dropping my luggage in my room, I decide to take a stroll along Orange Avenue to peruse the shops and restaurants. There are plenty of choices for a delicious lunch. This is such a great place.

A couple of hours later I amble down to the charming Glorietta Bay, and let the afternoon slip away on a bench at the yacht marina. Coronada is truly a slice of heaven.

At 6:00 pm, I meander along the beach, scanning for the luscious curves of my Tantrika.

A friendly wave in the distance.

My heart jumps.

I bound over and give her a big hug.

"It's so good to see you!"

She squeezes me affectionately.

Our fingers interlace as we walk along the water's edge.

An hour later, we are all caught up.

Silence settles upon us.

She points to a sand dune offering a wonderful vantage point to view the rippling ocean.

The sun is riding low and the sky is lighting up in orange and purple.

I was right. Truly spectacular.

She sighs contentedly.

"In the mood for a Tantra tutorial?"

"Thought you'd never ask."

"Alright. Where were we?"

Uh oh. Is this a test?

Snapping my fingers.

"Wait … oh yes …

"There are 4 key aspects of Tantra:

"Acceptance

"Openness

"Intimacy

"Energy"

Hmm … I should recapitulate.

"Let's start with **Acceptance**

"Acceptance is called self-love

"Acceptance is inward-directed

"Acceptance is saying 'I am OK'

"In Tantric terms, simply '**I Am**'"

She softly applauds.

I continue.

"The next one is **Openness**

"Openness is authenticity

"Openness is outward-directed

"Openness is saying 'I show freely'

"In Tantric terms, simply '**I Show**'"

I notice the serene smile.

She pats me on the leg.

"Let's discuss **Intimacy**

"Intimacy is an invitation

"Intimacy is other-directed

"Intimacy is saying 'I welcome you'

"In Tantric terms, simply '**I Welcome**'"

I am gazing at her earnestly.

"Intriguing ... tell me more."

She shifts her body position, then resumes.

"Intimacy is the natural sequel to openness.

"If you are open to a friend or romantic partner, it will encourage them to be open to you.

"Though you may have fears, you need to take the initiative.

"You need to risk your own openness and create opportunities for intimacy.

"Intimacy is an invitation to the other person.

"You are saying 'Show me your openness'

"You are saying 'Show me your authenticity'

"You are saying 'I accept you as you are'

"You are saying 'I welcome you in love'"

We watch two gulls flying wingtip to wingtip in the dusky sky.

Star-crossed lovers from another dimension.

The ambience is exquisilicious.

"You want to know the insight?"

"Yeah … apprise me."

"Intimacy.

"Into-me-I-see.

"Into-you-I-see.

"Boom!"

"I love it! Did you drop the mic again?"

She scans me seductively.

Excited butterflies flit in my tummy.

Place my hands on her cheeks.

Kiss her slowly in the soft light.

Wow. I want to make love right here.

Phew. Rein in these horses.

The sun has disappeared beneath the gentle waves.

A soft breeze is tickling our hair.

She cuddles close to me.

After a few minutes:

"Shall I say more?"

"Yes, please."

"Intimacy invites the romantic partner into the deepest core of your being. While it invites you into the deepest core of their being.

"Intimacy is only possible when you drop all your defences.

"When you discard your masks and compartments.

"When you risk your tender and vulnerable places."

My stomach clenches suddenly.

"Tender and vulnerable places?"

Sarita slides her hand onto mine.

"Yes, Allen. Deep intimacy allows wounds to rise.

"Wounds fester when they are repressed or hidden.

"Wounds heal when they are exposed to unconditional love.

"Deep intimacy is an opportunity for healing and freedom."

I feel a little apprehensive.

She smiles kindly at me.

"That brings us perfectly to the last aspect."

"Energy?"

"Indeed ...

"Let's talk about **Energy**

"Energy is a river of love

"Energy is circular-directed

"Energy is saying 'I flow with you'

"In Tantric terms, simply '**I Flow**'"

I unfold my arms and try to relax.

She pauses to ponder for a moment.

"You need to understand that Love is an energy, a state of being, not a *relationship*.

"Love is a river that flows. It is a moving entity. It is *relating*.

"Imagine a river flowing past a tree, nurturing its roots, then moving on. The river does not cling to the tree, negotiate the tree to stay, or ask for guarantees about the future.

"This, then, is Love."

The words of Sorcerer of the Heart cascade into my consciousness: 'You should be capable of being alone and blissful.

Then your love is *no longer a need but a sharing*. A sharing relationship is divine and exquisilicious.'

I feel Sarita's tender gaze upon me.

"What impedes the flow of the river?"

"Fear" erupts from my mouth.

"Touché, mon amour.

"The fundamental choice is always Love vs Fear.

"Fear drives you to seek certainty and predictability.

"Let's be clear: everyone needs the *security* of a home, job and financial income. That is a minimum requirement and necessary foundation for a calm and happy life.

"However, seeking *certainty* and *predictability* in relationships will not ensure happiness.

"Your romantic partner is alive and therefore unpredictable.

"People have ever-changing moods, needs and desires.

"Aliveness and predictability cannot coexist.

"If you stifle your partner, you stifle Love."

My head tilts thoughtfully.

"Blocking the river. Damming the river."

She nods and continues.

"Love is a flowing energy. Throw the word 'risk' away. 'Risk' exists solely because you seek certainty.

"Your partner is alive and constantly changes.

"There are no guarantees for the future.

"There can be no promises.

"Savour every moment.

"Stay in the present.

"Be here now.

"Surrender.

"Let go.

"Flow."

The light bulb turns on.

I truly understand the teachings.

Life is ... alive ... flowing ... uncertain ...

I need to fully inhabit each moment.

Be courageous and adventurous.

Flow with the river of Love.

Tantra has set me free.

I jump to my feet.

Pull her toward me.

Kiss her passionately.

Swaying in silver moonlight.

We snuggle into each other.

Feeling our heartbeats.

Merging energy fields.

"Sarita, is that a Tantric poem?"

Enquiring peek.

"I Am

"I Show

"I Welcome

"I Flow"

She raises her hand, opens her fingers.

"Boom."

* * *

Wowsers once more!

Sarita lives here in San Diego.

How cool is that?

Yummylicious Tantrika. Awesome city.

Life is kinda purrfect (yes, spelled that way).

We spend our weeks chasing the dream of Love.

Or more correctly, living each moment of Tantra.

"It's the full immersion, baby!" as she likes to say.

Every day I risk more (oops, forgive that word).

Sarita explained that Acceptance, Openness and Intimacy can be a gradual process.

It doesn't have to be all at once (is that even possible?).

As long as I am dedicated to surrendering, to deepening, to opening, to letting go ... then progress is made.

It is interesting.

A few wounds have surfaced.

I am being real and trusting.

Love seems to massage and heal.

It is a scary and beautiful thing.

I have to say *I love this city*.

First of all, the splendid weather.

You know the song 'It Never Rains in Southern California'?

It is gorgeously sunny almost every day.

Living near the coast is a Mediterranean lifestyle.

I adore being surrounded by the ocean.

And then there's the food.

Don't even get me started.

San Diego is renowned as one of America's best cities for 'foodies' (gastronomes). The culinary scene is a convergence of two styles: California cuisine, distinguished by fresh local ingredients and farm-to-table, and Mexico's Baja Med cuisine, which combines traditional Mexican and Mediterranean ingredients.

What's not to love?

Sarita and I spend much time in nature.

Apart from the sumptuous beaches there are fabulous parks.

The San Diego Botanic Garden in Encinitas offers 6 kilometres of garden trails, with an array of native and endangered plants, as well as the nation's largest collection of bamboo species.

Our favourite venue is Balboa Park.

Balboa Park features 16 unique gardens, including the Japanese Friendship Garden, the Inez Grant Parker Memorial Rose Garden (with over 2,400 rose bushes) and the Botanical Building (with over 2,100 plants, which include an enchanting collection of orchids, ferns, cycads and palms).

Balboa Park is also home to 17 museums, several performing arts venues, many cultural and recreational attractions, and the famous San Diego Zoo. While the San Diego Zoo Safari Park in Escondido is wonderful, the San Diego Zoo in Balboa Park is truly impressive. The San Diego Zoo has iconic status as the best zoo in the United States, and one of the finest zoos in the world.

Spread over 5 square kilometres, Balboa Park is the nation's largest urban cultural park.

After three months of ardent discussions, we make the big decision.

I move in with Sarita.

It requires some streamlining on my part.

Most of my books go into local storage.

She calls it 'Zenning'. It's a cute term.

It's about retaining only what you need.

Her house may be small but it's home.

We potter in the picturesque garden.

We dabble in part-time painting.

We attend local culinary classes.

Life is a blissful confluence …

Sunshine, beaches and nature.

Gastronomy and gardening.

Art and painting.

Love and Tantra.

A lot of Tantra.

* * *

Did I mention we do a lot of Tantra?

Yeah … I am smiling right now.

Tantra is a way of life.

A blissful lifestyle.

Yes, it is about spirit, energy and chakras.

Yes, it is about mind and emotions.

Yes, it is all about love.

And it is about sex.

Mind-blowing sex.

Ohhh-M-G sex.

Is that a smile?

A glint in your eye?

Here's the thing:

You need to master Acceptance, Openness, Intimacy and Energy to truly appreciate and experience great sex.

There is also something special about practicing Tantra with your romantic partner.

I am grateful that Sarita pushed me to read the books Star Child and The Tribe.

They provided the deep metaphysical background to Tantra, as well as some crucial pragmatic guidelines.

Once the spiritual, psychological and emotional foundation is built, you can move onto awesome, delicious and divine sex.

Sarita has taught me how to be free.

I often give her hour-long orgasms.

Yep, you read that correctly.

Orgasms are fascinating.

They can occur in one or more chakras (each with its own delectable flavour, feeling and texture).

They can occur in the entire body and or energy field.

They can be localised in the genitals and or anus.

And there is the incredible Kundalini orgasm.

I have now experienced all of those.

It is interesting where the challenges lay.

Energy blockages impede sexual energy.

You may have to do chakra healing.

You may have to heal your past.

You may have to free your mind.

I happily became adept at the C-spot (clitoris; usually essential for great orgasms) and G-spot (Gräfenberg spot; a bean-shaped area of the vagina, which in *some* females causes powerful orgasms and ejaculation).

I flinched when Sarita introduced the topic of anal stimulation.

She patiently explained that the anus is rich with sensory nerve endings. Like the vagina, most of those nerve endings are concentrated around the opening and just inside.

The anus (and perineum) can be a site of sexual pleasure for any gender or sexual orientation. (Unfortunately, misguided beliefs and sexual stigmas – e.g. a straight man believing he is homosexual or fearing being labelled homosexual – cause many people to shy away from anal stimulation.)

I also learned about the P-spot (prostate gland; a sensory walnut-sized gland in males that is accessible via the anus). Caressing or massaging the prostate can produce mind-blowing orgasms.

Important side note: Regular prostate massages are an essential health practice, especially for men over the age of 35. The benefits of prostate massage (aka 'milking'):

Supports healthy prostate functioning.
Improves and heightens sexual experience.
Prevents build up of prostatic fluid in prostate.
Helps prevent BPH, also known as enlarged prostate.
Reduces pain and discomfort of an inflamed prostate.
Improves effectiveness of antibiotics against prostatitis.

As always, you need to do your research, heed medical guidelines, and discover what works best for your body.

I have a sexy Tantrika for a partner.

There are times when I combine anal stimulation with clitoral and or vaginal stimulation (obviously never using the same finger for the front and back). It is usually best to wait for her request. She knows when her body wants it.

When my body is in the mood, I enjoy a gentle well-lubricated finger. (Most people prefer no more than one finger, two at most. Anything larger may feel uncomfortable or painful.)

If you are feeling really adventurous, a flat sensual 'ice-cream' tongue caressing the anus can be a divine experience. (That is known as 'analingus'.)

Phew. How my life as changed ...

My Tantrika often reminds me:

"Surrender and flow, baby!"

Tantra is about intimacy.

Psychological intimacy.

Emotional intimacy.

Spiritual intimacy.

Physical intimacy.

Intimacy brings you closer to your partner.

Strengthens the connection between you.

Creates waves of deep fulfilment.

Ensconces you in bliss.

Wraps you in Love.

* * *

I've been ignoring the magick book.

Life has been sweet in this world.

My evolution has progressed.

Enormous leaps and bounds.

Embracing the path of Tantra.

Still practicing Awareness.

Enfolded in Love.

Now it is time.

Deep breaths.

Book in my lap.

Tickle the ornate stitching.

A glowing icon … shaggy umbrella?

Burning my right thigh.

Explosion of light.

Multicoloured vortex.

Intense scchhh sound …

A golden doorway appears.

I bow to the maroon-clad lama.

We exchange the Tashi Delek greeting.

"Welcome to Drepung Monastery in Lhasa, Tibet. The name Drepung means 'rice heap' which comes from the Sanskrit Dhanyakataka, the name of a stupa in south India where the Buddha first taught the Kalachakra Tantra. Drepung is the site of the burial stupas of the 2nd, 3rd and 4th Dalai Lamas (only the Potala Palace has more burial stupas of Dalai Lamas)."

"I am honoured to be here."

He scrutinises my energy field.

"You have come far, grasshopper. Soon we will call you locust."

The inane joke somehow makes me laugh.

Unless … is it referring to evolution?

Is it about ascending levels?

I ponder for a moment.

"Shall I explain your tattoo?"

"That would be great."

He smiles knowingly.

"The Victory Banner is an Auspicious Symbol. In classic Buddhism it represents the Buddha's victory over the four maras, or hindrances on the path to enlightenment. However, if you want the shortcut version, here's a simple analogy …"

Long-lasting pause.

"Yes …?"

He claps his hands dramatically.

"Life is a banana peeling a monkey."

I burst into laughter.

"Exactly."

"Is that a mantra or something?"

"You graduate when you understand."

Rubbing my chin curiously.

"Um … can you give me a clue?"

He studies me intently.

"Don't take it seriously.

"It's just a cosmic play.

"Learn to dance.

"Celebrate.

"Be joyful.

"Breathe.

"Love.

"Live."

I am contemplating his words.

"Cease seeking. Begin living."

I feel the swift slap on my back.

Hurtling through the vortex.

Amid raucous laughter, I hear:

"May the Buddha Force be with you."

I land back in our bedroom.

Sarita is reposing on the chaise longue.

"How was the trip, honey?"

Admiring her radiant face.

"Come here, you ..."

Take her in my arms.

Holding her close.

Energy fields melting.

"I love you

"Truly

"Madly

"Deeply

"Always."

Soft purring.

"Always."

* * *

Sarita and I are walking in a beautiful forest.

Trees are whispering around us.

Birds are softly tweeting.

Sunlight tickles our skin.

She first notices the purple coat.

I narrow my eyes to see in the distance.

Her voice is dulcet.

"It's Michael."

Crunch of almost-black combat boots.

Allen. Sarita.

I frown quickly.

"You know each other?"

"Of course, silly."

Protracted exhale.

"It's been a long time."

Michael nods affably.

"What brings you here?"

My tone sounds a bit harsh.

What's wrong with me?

Am I feeling territorial?

How bizarre.

A blazing smile.

I've come to take you home.

"Both of us?" I blurt.

He looks at me curiously.

Your paths are intertwined.

I will not disrupt Love.

Sudden sense of relief.

Sarita reaches for my hand.

"Surrender and flow, my love."

I exhale consciously and calm down.

"It's all going to be ok."

Michael signals to the sky.

A powerful vortex opens above us.

I am going to show you a glimpse.

You will decide how to proceed.

It's going to be your choice.

I am feeling much better.

Vivid colours envelop us.

Familiar scchhh sound ...

Glistening white doorway.

Shimmering mist before us.

Surrounded by steep snow-capped mountains.

Moving steadily along the stark path.

We pass the desolate rock face ...

Arrive in a lush green valley ...

Profusion of bright flowers ...

Huge monastery revealed ...

I can't wait any longer.

"Where are we?"

Michael gestures expansively.

The Magick Kingdom in Tibet.

"The what-now?"

Let me paint the canvas for you.

We sit at his feet and listen.

In the ancient Tibetan Shangshung scriptures, and the Kalachakra Tantra, there is mention of 7 hidden lands located on this Earth.

Each sacred land is hidden in a boundless valley (beyul), and protected by fiery dragons, ethereal mists and supernatural snowstorms.

Known only to initiated lamas and recorded on secret scrolls, these lands remain hidden from the rest of the world.

"What is the name of this place?"

He gazes slowly across the landscape.

Shambhala (aka the Magick Kingdom in Tibet).

Bön scriptures called it Tagsig Olmo Lung Ring.

Sarita is fascinated by her surroundings.

She asks: "What is the purpose? Why was it created?"

Each hidden land is a dual dimension, where the physical and spiritual worlds exist in perfect harmony.

Michael shrugs insouciantly.

You could say it's where Heaven meets Earth ... or to be precise, the intersection of a heaven and Earth.

"A higher dimension blending with a lower dimension?"

That's close enough.

"Awesome."

I frown inquisitively.

"Who lives here?"

Peal of joyful laughter.

Apart from the fiery dragons and inconspicuous snow leopards?

"Uh, yeah ..."

Shambhala is home to the 'Shining Ones'.

Awakened shaman-monks and sorcerers who have dedicated themselves to perfecting their art and protecting the Earth.

"Shining Ones?"

Luminous powerful energy fields.

"Aha."

Do you recall the different manifestations of sorcery?

Scratching my head.

Sarita astutely interjects.

"A sorcerer learns the mystical skill and art. She blends that with her temperament, disposition, knowledge and passions. Each sorcerer finds her own expression. Some walk the path of Shamanism. Some surrender into deepest Awareness. Others immerse entirely into Love. Still others blossom into tantalising Tantrikas. The sorcerer also aligns to the Light or the Dark. All that dictates the type of work she will do, and the lifestyle she will lead."

Perfectly recited.

She stares at him curiously.

How do you gain access to Shambhala?

She contemplates for a moment.

"Align to the Light."

Yes, and ...?

"Immerse into Love."

Do you think you both qualify?

I glance at Sarita and smile.

"Absolutely."

The Shining Ones are bearers of great wisdom ... masters of chi ... energy healers ... yogis ... interdimensional travellers.

If you reside here, you will make rapid progress.

Are you interested in living in Shambhala?

We both nod solemnly.

I notice our dragons hovering in the distance, along with an immense dragon who is connected to Michael.

Our dragons, you remember, are called Blaze and Glow.

Michael's dragon is Lumen (ultra cool name). I consult the Oxford Concise English Dictionary on my phone: 'Lumen is the SI unit of luminous flux, equal to the amount of light emitted per second in a unit solid angle of one steradian from a uniform source of one candela.' Whaaaat? Yeah, but it sounds impressive.

Turns out that Lumen is an exceptionally powerful shapeshifting hummingbird. An 'Avatar' or catalyst of the universe.

I sigh quietly. So much to learn.

As Michael invites us to return to San Diego, I ask him a pointed question:

"Where is Shambhala on a map?"

He stares at me blankly.

You understand it's a secret?

"Yes ..."

All I can tell you is it's near sacred Mount Kailash and holy Lake Manasarovar.

He covers his mouth, squeezes his eyes.

Ngari!shhh

"Bless you."

We cascade through the vortex.

Arrive back in the beautiful forest.

Michael smiles knowingly.

You have much to discuss.

Our heads bob in unison.

If you want to make the shift ...

Open the magick book together ...

You'll both need the twelfth tattoo.

It grants full access to Shambhala.

His purple robe dazzles with Light.

It's covered in Auspicious Symbols.

Scintillating and intriguing!

A flourish, and he is gone.

* * *

We take a few days to absorb the experience.

It is at once exciting and mysterious.

Yet we are filled with trepidation.

How will our lives change?

What will we give up?

What will we lose?

I find myself consoling Sarita.

Then a few hours later she is consoling me.

Seems a bigger decision than we anticipated.

Thing is, we have just settled into a home life.

Into a new routine; into a particular lifestyle.

Neither one of us wants to be uprooted.

This harks back to the discussion on security.

Sarita's previous words: '... everyone needs the *security* of a home, job and financial income. That is a minimum requirement and necessary foundation for a calm and happy life.'

In Shambhala, food is abundant and accommodation is free.

We will be ensconced in magick, knowledge and power.

We won't need income streams.

Goodbye vexatious capitalism.

So what is holding us back?

Eventually, it drops into our consciousness.

It's the gorgeous blue ocean that we adore.

Intermingled in the fabric of our souls.

How can we live without that?

We decide to take a few weeks.

Let things integrate and settle.

Enjoy plenty of beach time ...

Scrunch into golden sand ...

Savour the ocean breeze ...

Swim the azure waters ...

Let it all naturally unfold.

After a month, we are tetchy.

Know that feeling when a door has closed ... and you haven't moved on yet?

It starts to get uncomfortable.

I adopt a positive attitude.

If I am to be surrounded by advanced knowledge, then my book collection is redundant (at very least).

It takes a few phone calls; my books are gratefully collected by specialist stores.

This inspires the woman I love.

Her energy shifts dramatically.

I cannot resist commenting:

"Nothing like Zenning!"

Her house is quickly sold.

Possessions are given away.

Soon we own ... nothing.

Farewells are uttered.

On the last day, at sunset, we head to Coronado Beach.

We lay out the large picnic blanket.

Gaze at the unfurling waves.

Then consciously breathe.

Briefly close our eyes.

A muted "au revoir".

* * *

The sunset is spectacular.

A serene ambience settles.

I gesture at the magick book.

"Would you like to activate it?"

Sarita tickles the ornate stitching.

It flips open straight away.

A glowing icon is revealed.

We place our palms down.

Burning our left shoulders.

Explosion of brightest light.

Colourful vortex envelops us.

An ancient wooden doorway.

Maroon-clad lama at the grey steps.

We are outside the huge monastery.

I hear Sarita's exclamation:

"Sorcerer of the Heart!"

Knew I'd see him again.

"Welcome, newbies."

We do our best Namaste bows.

"You have both acquired your twelfth tattoo.

"The Eternal Knot (aka Endless Knot) is an Auspicious Symbol. It represents the confluence of time and movement; the intertwining of wisdom and compassion; the merging of Awareness and Love.

"It depicts the interweaving of spirituality and pragmatism; the integration of mystical dimensions and mundane planes; the unity of the manifested and unmanifested.

"It is the Divine and Eternal."

I glance at the magnificent building.

The sorcerer bounces an imaginary basketball then throws it.

"The tattoo allows you to live in Shambhala."

We hear a resounding "Boomshakalaka!"

A smile lights up my face.

He points to the lush valley.

"A wonderful house awaits you."

Sarita whispers contentedly.

"What will we do in Shambhala?"

He pauses for a long time, as if assessing us.

"You do whatever makes you happy."

"Aren't we supposed to serve the world?"

"You give when you are overflowing."

He places his palms on his heart chakra.

"Fill your hearts and souls first."

"And then we will save the world?"

He gazes tenderly at Sarita.

"Live for yourselves first.

"Create your home.

"Build a rich life.

"Live for Love."

He bends to caress a flower.

"Presence of Heart.

"That's the key.

"The rest will flow.

"Naturally."

I am smiling again.

Another Tantric poem?

"If you ever get out to the world, don't be a reformer, don't try to change others, don't try to save others. If you bring your Heart energy, that's enough of a message."

I feel an anxious pang.

"When will we meet the others?"

The sorcerer stares at me intently.

"All the lamas who taught you are here.

"Many advanced souls reside here.

"Just be. You will find each other.

"Although all the dragons ascended to Michael's world a long time ago, the cosmic intersection allows them into the 7 hidden lands.

"The dragons are your teachers and protectors.

"The snow leopards are also your protectors.

"You might even encounter a unicorn."

I contemplate his guidance, then:

"Is there an overarching plan?"

He smiles sagaciously.

"Cosmic chessboard.

"Moving advanced souls into pivotal positions.

"To spread more Light through the Darkness."

It makes sense.

I feel at peace.

Bowing to Sorcerer of the Heart.

Taking Sarita's hand in mine.

Walking toward our new house.

As we amble past the little temple, I notice the inscription:

Ask not 'Who am I?' as it implies identity. Ask 'What am I?' which leads to Consciousness.

I shrug innocently. That's for the next esoteric book.

Faint music emanates from a slightly open window.

The song is Almost Unreal by Roxette.

I catch a few lyrics.

'Fate did arrange
For us to meet
I love when you do
That hocus pocus to me
The way that you touch
You've got the power to heal
You give me that look
It's almost unreal
Sometimes I feel
Strange as it seems
You've been in my dreams
All my life ...'

Blue and white butterflies are dancing delicately around us. A soft breeze is fluttering the grass. Birds are murmuring and gently nuzzling in the trees. A full moon is mystically rising and splashing silver across our new home.

Stars are twinkling brightly.

I gaze into Sarita's eyes.

It's all kinda purrfect.

Sorcery of the Heart.

Dance of Magick.

Tantra Love.

Stephen Shaw's Books

Visit the website: www.i-am-stephen-shaw.com

I Am contains spiritual and mystical teachings from enlightened masters that point the way to love, peace, bliss, freedom and spiritual awakening.

Heart Song takes you on a mystical adventure into creating your reality and manifesting your dreams, and reveals the secrets to attaining a fulfilled and joyful life.

They Walk Among Us is a love story spanning two realities. Explore the mystery of the angels. Discover the secrets of Love Whispering.

The Other Side explores the most fundamental question in each reality. What happens when the physical body dies? Where do you go? Expand your awareness. Journey deep into the Mystery.

Reflections offers mystical words for guidance, meditation and contemplation. Open the book anywhere and unwrap your daily inspiration.

5D is the Fifth Dimension. Discover ethereal doorways hidden in the fabric of space-time. Seek the advanced mystical teachings.

Star Child offers an exciting glimpse into the future on earth. The return of the gods and the advanced mystical teachings. And the ultimate battle of light versus darkness.

The Tribe expounds the joyful creation of new Earth. What happened after the legendary battle of Machu Picchu? What is Christ consciousness? What is Ecstatic Tantra?

The Fractal Key reveals the secrets of the shamans. This handbook for psychonauts discloses the techniques and practices used in psychedelic healing and transcendent journeys.

Stephen Shaw's Books

Atlantis illuminates the Star Beings and Earth's Ancient History. A magical history ingrained in your deepest consciousness, in your myths and mysteries. Discover the secret teachings of the star beings.

The Sorcerer is a journey into Magick, Power and Mysticism. Discover the Twelve Auspicious Symbols. Explore the paths of Awareness, Love and Tantra. Absorb the sacred teachings and mantras of the lamas.